Sit Down,

Shut Up,

You're Gonna Win This Thing

Dave Greenberg

Published in the United States by Mimo Publishing, New Jersey.

ISBN: 1-7323642-0-6
ISBN-13: 978-1-7323642-0-2

First Paperback Edition

For Travis

Dedicated to the reader battling bravely

With eternal gratitude to Mom & Dad

"Luck is what happens when preparation meets opportunity."

-Seneca

CONTENTS

PART II: Opportunity

PART III: Transforming Luck

Prologue

"This guy's walking down the street when he falls in a hole. The walls are so steep he can't get out. A doctor passes by and the guy shouts up, 'Hey you. Can you help me out?' The doctor writes a prescription, throws it down in the hole and moves on. Then a priest comes along and the guy shouts up, 'Father, I'm down in this hole can you help me out?' The priest writes out a prayer, throws it down in the hole and moves on. Then a friend walks by, 'Hey, Joe, it's me can you help me out?' And the friend jumps in the hole. Our guy says, 'Are you stupid? Now we're both down here.' The friend says, 'Yeah, but I've been down here before and I know the way out.'"

—Leo's Story & Other Stories and Writings

This quote establishes what I hope to give back to the reader. In #32 Noël of *The West Wing*, Leo tells Josh the above story. (Josh refers to it when talking to Leo in "Bartlet for America"). I hope to be Joe for you. I may not have been stuck in the specific hole you find yourself in right now, but I have found myself trapped at the bottom of my fair share of abysses, and I've learned a thing or two on my way out of each one of them. Moreover, some of the falls and failings have led to some of my greatest successes. It is my hope to share with you what I've learned about how to turn a negative situation into a strength and perhaps entertain you along the way. Most important—I want you to know you're not alone in what you're going through. This book will not have all the answers to all of your problems, but I hope it serves as an inspirational hand, lifting you out of that hole.

Part 1

Preparation

One

(You Gotta) Fight for Your Right (To ~~Party~~ Fight)

There I was at the back of a line, waiting to enter an underground club in New York City. It was Adam's twenty-sixth birthday—a pretty inconsequential age to drag so many of us out. Nerd alert: Adam and I met in the gifted and talented program at nine years of age. It wasn't until the following year when we had the same mainstream teacher that we became genuinely close. From that point forward, he became one of my unwavering best friends. There were about thirty of us out for Adam that night. I remember thinking to myself, *I am one fortunate guy to have such a close network of true friends.* Really, the occasion could have been nice weather on a Saturday night to get us all together at this brilliant age.

As I was saying, I was last on a line that curved down a dimly lit flight of stairs leading to a set of four large doors with four equally large bouncers holding their posts in front of each. They were wearing all black, and yet they were still better dressed than me—fashion had never been my strong suit, and being a broke graduate student certainly wasn't lending any favors to my style. The fashion-forward bouncers were patting down everyone before allowing entry. I remember thinking that I had never been searched to enter a club before. Do fights really happen with such a security presence? Besides noting the oddity, I didn't think much of it. Perhaps it was the couple of "pregame" drinks I'd had earlier, or maybe it was just my boy-like immaturity, but as one of the giant bouncers was patting me down, checking for weapons, I couldn't help but think to myself: *I am my own weapon.* Amused by my silly thought, I smiled wryly as I entered the club through those oversized doors and beyond those oversized bouncers.

Chris was the one who put this night together and was, without a doubt, the organizer of our group. Chris was also one of my best friends, with our friendship spanning just as long as Adam's and mine. Chris' sister Cathy was out with us too. Once inside the club for a bit, Cathy, one of her friends, and I were being playful with one another. Next to us there was an oversized chair (a throne really) which becomes a good centerpiece for our lightheartedness. My friends and, by extension, my friends' friends, often joke with me about how my ego has me thinking that I'm a superhero (they're not wrong). Cathy and her friend took the low-lying fruit and teased me that the throne must have been placed there beforehand with the knowledge I would be frequenting these parts. Lately, my endeavor to become a mixed martial artist had provided my friends more material with which to roast me. The girls beckoned me to sit on the throne for my picture to be snapped. I wouldn't do it though.

"You can take a before picture of me *next* to the throne, but I won't sit in it until I win a fight."

"What if you never fight?" they asked in unison.

"Then I'll never have earned my spot on the throne."

I was happily drinking and enjoying my time with everyone celebrating Adam's birthday. Upon a bit of a lull in the conversation, I reflexively checked my phone for texts and e-mails. In the preceding weeks, I had been in correspondence with a fight promoter trying to book my first mixed martial arts (MMA) fight. I had been trying to book a fight since February, and Adam's birthday was in the middle of May. There had been two previous failed attempts, with two distinct promotions. The feeling that I was too green and my dream of fighting would never come to fruition had started to infiltrate my psyche. The latest correspondence with this third fight promotion had left off with the promoter asking me for my fight experience and credentials. Despite doing my best to boost what little experience I had, I still was not confident it would be enough to earn the booking. I had tried to make up for my lacking credentials with a humorous and likable personality. When he asked me by email what experience I had, I answered that I had not yet taken a martial arts class.

"Should you give me the opportunity to fight, would you kindly also pass along some fight schools you would recommend for me to start training?"

Immediately after, I informed him that I was only kidding and provided him the list of my credentials.

Now back at Adam's celebration, I looked down at my phone and indeed had received a response from the fight promoter. It read:

"Great sense of humor. You're in."

I must have done three or four double takes. I couldn't believe what I was reading. Honest to God it felt like a dream come true. Immediately after, I lost my cool.

"I booked a fight!" I exclaimed to the bartender.

It was loud in the club, and he must have asked me three or four times what it was I was saying. I kept yelling to him that I had booked a fight. On the last one, his face went from quizzical to stern and serious.

"You want to fight me?!"

"No, no, no, I booked a fight in Atlantic City!" I chuckled.

He instantly relaxed. "Congrats. Let me get you a drink on the house."

"Thanks! Club soda please."

A switch had been flipped, and everything I did from that point forward would be with the focus of doing everything right for the fight. No more alcohol for me. I could not contain my excitement and began letting out cries of elation to all of my friends.

"Look at my phone! Look at my phone!"

One by one my friends started catching wind that something was going on and started to make their way over to me.

I kept asking my friends, "Am I dreaming? It feels like I'm dreaming!"

Another one of my longtime best friends Brad, kept reassuring me, "It's real man. It's real."

As Brad was assuring me, my friend Matt made his way over to see what all the commotion was about. Matt must have been jealous, and probably a little drunk. Without saying a word, he sauntered over to me and swatted my phone out of my hand. Now, this act alone would have been enough to piss me off, but being a broke grad student, my new smartphone was one of my nicest possessions. This exacerbated my anger.

"What the hell man?!"

With a dopy grin, he asked, "What are you gonna do about it?"

"How about I kick your ass?"

Just then our friend Lisa stepped in between us, pleading for us to stop and calm down. I obliged even though Matt deserved a good old-fashioned ass-whooping. I went to track down my phone, and to my surprise and delight, it was undamaged. Now happy again, I began to show the rest of my friends my great news. Then almost beyond belief, Matt makes his way back over to me, and this time smacks my phone clear across the bar. Scathing mad doesn't even begin to capture the sort of anger that washed over me.

"What?! I'm not scared of you," Matt challenged.

"Yeah? Well, you should be!" I cringed a little inside in recognition of the Spaghetti Western cliché I had just uttered.

Right about this time, despite being scorching mad, is when I had a vision of how things out of my control could end my dream before it had really even gotten off the ground. I could see my head hitting the bar in an ensuing melee. I could see strangers getting involved and my face being busted open by some random drunkard swinging a bar stool.

"So, what's stopping you? Come and kick my ass," Matt taunted.

Armed with my vision of losing everything I had wanted, worked for, and had just been granted being stripped away by some foolish freak accident, I had the presence of mind to cool my jets.

"Listen up jerk, and listen good. When *you* are good enough to fight in Atlantic City—I'll kick your ass there."

Well, I cooled my jets enough to not kick his ass anyway. I spent the rest of the night avoiding Matt. All of the girls we were out with kept finding me in the corner of the club I had tucked myself away into. They were trying to get me to come out on to the dance floor and dance with them. I would have none of that. I was completely content to ride out the rest of the night. I was already looking forward to the next day. I was anxious to start figuring out the logistics of my training camp. At the top of my new to-do list was to figure out how to tell my trainer that I booked a fight. Usually, it was your trainer that booked the fight, not the fighter. I decided it would probably be best for me to start training again consistently before I broke the news to him.

Two

New York City Aftermath

As if all the drama at the club for Adam's birthday wasn't enough, that night was far from over. While I was holed up in some corner avoiding fighting Matt, my friend, Seth, (a slender, slightly neurotic, highly sarcastic, peaceable guy) got into it with one of the bouncers and was forcibly removed from the club. There was a lot of drama revolving around his extrication that I don't fully remember. Anyway, it was time for me start making my way back to my friends, Chris' and Brad's apartment, where I'd be crashing for the night. I was taking that journey back with Chris, who was quite inebriated and on the receiving end of a few rejections from women, probably due to his level of drunkenness. Needless to say, this put Chris in a bit of a sour mood. Stepping in between a few would-be fights with ticked off boyfriends, and corralling him from the busy New York City streets, and we were back to his place. It was late, and I was drained from all of the evening's events. I promptly fell asleep on their couch only to be woken up moments later by Chris' punch straight to my face. After a quick skirmish and a swiftly executed submission, Chris ceased his attack and I fell back asleep.

The next morning, we all woke up a bit hung over (me less so thanks to converting to club sodas). Eric, another dear friend of mine in the group, was sharing the couch next to mine, and we could tell he was hiding something behind his smirk. Turns out he had a couple of things on his mind: the first was that I had dried blood on my face that looked like I had cried a single blood tear (thanks to Chris' surprise wakeup call in the middle of the night). After washing my face, we pressed Eric for what else he was holding. Apparently, in the middle of the night, I had woken up to go to the bathroom. Only, I didn't use the bathroom. According to Eric, through his laughs, I had walked over to the couch next to the one I had been sleeping on and proceeded to initiate relieving my bladder. Eric had woken up from the commotion I must have made and had seen me standing over him in an awkwardly threatening position. "Hey Dave, what's going on?" Without so much as a word, I had let her rip. Eric said he had narrowly dodged my stream by springing off the couch. Guess I hadn't switched over to those club sodas soon enough. I offered Chris to pay to have the couch cleaned (even after the drunken assault on me). Chris

8

reassured me that was unnecessary as I was not the first to relieve myself on that couch. Poor Eric.

The group rallied to go out and get breakfast in a nice open-air courtyard-type restaurant in the heart of hipster-ville. Once we ordered, we all retreated to our phones, and Matt noticed the shattered screen on mine.

"What happened to your phone?" he asked.

"Really?"

Matt responded with an honest look. "Yeah, what happened?"

"Matt, you did that at the bar last night. You knocked it out of my hands—twice actually."

Matt, feeling ashamed, immediately promised he would replace it, and that he was sorry. I was surprised how honorable Matt was in owning up to his misbehavior. Moreover, Matt proved to be a man of his word as he did in fact replace a not so cheap iPhone.

I was anxious to get back home in order to restructure my life and focus in on the training. Home had been my particularly wealthy and generous cousin's mansion for the last couple of years in central New Jersey. John, my best friend since I was 10 years old, was living in North Jersey. On my way home, I decided to stop and share my good news with him. Though by the time I had gotten there, my news had already preceded me. Adam couldn't contain his excitement and spilled the beans. No matter, John's excitement was made clear through his sincere smile. I opened up to him and his fiancée, Mel, about something I was keeping for myself on some level.

"I was starting to believe that I would never in fact realize my dream of fighting in a venue like an Atlantic City Casino."

Without skipping a beat, John said earnestly and confidently, "I always knew you would realize your dream." Sensing my anxiousness to begin, John promptly kicked me out of his house to allow me to properly prepare for what I had just gotten myself into.

"Get after it, Meanberg." John used the playful nickname he came up with when I protested his original suggestion of "Mean" Dave Greenberg. He liked it because it rhymed. I informed him it didn't rhyme. A spark of genius and self-amusement came over his face when he came up with "Meanberg" to satisfy my rhyming requirement. It's always the nicknames we don't want that are the ones that stick.

Three

Breaking News…and My Arm

So, I have a confession to make: I had taken a break from training. A long break. I had sort of been training. That is to say maybe I had trained between six and eight times in the previous couple of months. The frequency of training I would need to ramp up to would require training two to four time per *day,* six days per week. Given my extended absence, I decided it was probably best I was somewhat consistent before I broke the news of booking a fight to my trainer. I had broken the cardinal rule by booking the fight myself. Making matters worse, I booked it without any communication with my trainer. Usually the order of things is as such:

1. Let your trainer know you are interested in having a fight
2. Your trainer provides you an honest assessment of where your skill level is at
3. Working together, you come up with a timeline
4. Establish check-in points to see how you're progressing
5. Only after all previous steps were met would your trainer check in with you before *he* booked the fight

Somewhere along the way I learned that it's easier to ask for forgiveness than it is to get permission. Again the plan was to get a couple of weeks' worth of training and then tell my trainer. The first of a series of challenges that tested how badly I wanted that fight cropped up in that very first week back training. A major part of my training consisted of Brazilian Jiu-Jitsu (BJJ)—a submission grappling martial art form. It's a derivative of traditional Japanese Jiu-Jitsu, where the founder, Grand Master Relio Gracie, adapted the teachings to suit his small and weaker-bodied frame. It's very similar to wrestling. The major difference being, where in wrestling the aim is to pin your opponent's shoulder blades to the ground, in BJJ the major objective is to submit your opponent primarily through various chokes and joint locks (forcing a joint to go against the opposite way it was intended to move). To keep things safe in training and even in competition, a "tap out" was implemented to communicate to your opponent that they were successful in their attack and you give up. If the offensive competitor were to continue, you would go unconscious from their choke or have your joint broken from their lock.

Often times while training, different skill-leveled partners (denoted by the color of their belt) get paired up with one another. Similarly, different-sized training partners also are paired up in training. So, nothing was out of the ordinary when my instructor paired me up with a 6'0" 275 lbs. student who was a whole belt level more advanced than me. For the record, I was about 5'8" and 170 lbs. There were intangibles at play while training as well: tenaciousness, athleticism, craftiness, and grit to name a few.

For the most part, I was able to hang with my training partner thanks to those intangibles—until I couldn't. I got caught in an arm lock submission where my training partner was trying to force my elbow to go the opposite direction as intended. I was defending adequately. I wasn't troubled by the submission itself that I was trapped in. Rather while fighting the submission, mine and my partner's relative positions were abruptly and violently shifted. All of the combined weight of my opponent's body and my own concentrated pressure on my already vulnerable and trapped elbow. *Pop!* Just like that my elbow hyperextended.

Grittiness is an advantageous trait to have while training martial arts—most of the time. Grit will be somewhat of a theme throughout this book, and make no mistake about it: I credit it for many of my achievements. However, in this particular case, it may have been expressed in a less than productive way. Perhaps, I'm merely confusing grit with my stubbornness. Either way, as it played out in one of my first training sessions back, despite having my elbow audibly hyperextended, I fought through it to complete (and win) the training round.

Four

Coincidence or Omen

Knocked off my cloud, I went to the hospital. I was scared that the injury might preclude me from fighting. I knew I would fight injured if I had to, but I also knew I would need the doctor's clearance. I realized then I did not have total control of all outcomes. I decided I would focus all my efforts on the elements in my training I did have control over. In that moment, though, I found myself hopeful for the things I had no control over.

A little context is in order for what was to come next. At this time in my life I was living with my generous, smart, competitive, and wealthy cousin and his awesome family. My cousin Eric had been a mentor and strong role model of mine since early childhood. Eric had taught me how to ski and play chess when I had been only five-years-old. He has taught me much more since then, and I still look up to him. While living with Eric, he introduced me to TED Talks, before they were as well-known as they are now. TED Talks provide a platform for the best and brightest minds, spanning many disciplines to present their findings in their given area of study. I gorged myself on those talks. They can pique your interest in a given subject, but because the talks are between five minutes and half an hour, they can also leave you thirsty for more. I was impressed with Simon Sinek's talk, "How Great Leaders Inspire Action." I wanted to learn more and so bought his book, *Start with Why: How Great Leaders Inspire Everyone to Take Action.*

Back at the hospital, I figured I would need something to entertain myself as I waited for who knew how long at the emergency room to have my elbow checked out. After checking in, I sat on one of the uncomfortable chairs in the waiting room and began to read the Sinek book to pass the time. I couldn't have been reading for more than five minutes before the attractive administrative assistant came racing over to me. Without warning, she ripped the book out of my hand. Wide-eyed and surprised, I must have shot her a pretty quizzical look. After realizing what she had just done, she quickly explained, "I thought that was Simon Sinek." (His picture was on the back cover.)

"Oh, you must be a really big fan of his I guess," I said, slightly deflated that she wasn't rushing over for me.

"Well yes, no—I don't know. I didn't know he wrote a book. I dated him in high school."

What are the odds of that? I thought to myself. After a couple of more pleasant exchanges, she went back behind her desk. I decided to take it as a good omen, as it happened right after the realization I wasn't going to be able to control all aspects of my journey to my first cage fight. And wouldn't you know it, my elbow was only sprained.

Five

On/Off to a Dimmer

Confession time again: I had never actually sparred in an MMA format before I booked my fight. Heck, I never really ever sparred in any context, unless you consider grappling to be sparring. It was probably a good thing I still had not told my trainer that I'd booked that fight yet, before I had shown up to his invite-only sparring class. Here again I benefited from the quote, "It is easier to ask for forgiveness than it is to get permission." One of the greatest strengths of the martial arts academy I trained at was the caliber of my training partners. There was a wide breadth of experience in the training room ranging from former college wrestlers, high-level Brazilian Jiu-Jitsu practitioners, professional boxers, professional Muay Thai kickboxers, and most importantly amateur and professional mixed martial artists. So, you can imagine the nerves I was feeling before entering that first sparring session, especially never having been invited.

To this day I am still not quite sure how to gauge my intensity level when it comes to sparring. Sparring is quite close to fighting, but it is not fighting. Some see sparring and fighting as different points on the same spectrum. Thus, some can dial in their intensity like a dimmer switch. I'm not like that. For me that switch is either on or off. If someone punches me to the point of pain, instinctually I want to ramp up my intensity to a 10. The blows have to be real to simulate a fighting environment, but not to the point of injuring your training partner. Like anything else, the more I did it, the better I got at it. After two solid weeks back training and now sparring, I was beginning to work up the nerve to tell my trainer that I booked a fight. At least that is what I was telling myself.

Six

The First Glimmer

MMA sparring took some getting used to. By that I mean I took some serious beatings. Sparring professional mixed martial artists for the first time was like learning to walk for the first time—while getting punched in the face repeatedly. My strategy was merely to survive, and somehow I did. I'll tell you what though, my defensive skills were getting a real workout. While not for everyone, diving into the deep end and figuring it out is how I learn best. I have found few things that sharpen senses and hasten learning more than hand-to-hand combat.

The *only* reason I developed any skills at all, is because I kept showing up when training got this hard. I would take my beatings, nurse them afterward, and most importantly show up the next day. How bad were the beatings? I literally would not be able to move most of my joints due to all the swelling caused by the strikes I was absorbing. I had to learn the value of taking care of myself. I iced my injuries religiously. After icing my injuries and a full night of rest, I would regain about half of the mobility and functionality. Running and stretching in the morning helped me to recover further before my martial arts training in the evening. One day after paying many dues, I had one fleeting moment of success. I was taking my usual beating from our best-striking professional mixed martial artist. In the middle of the round, I ducked one of his punches and transitioned into taking him down. I was like a puppy who actually caught the mail truck he had been chasing forever and then didn't know what to do with it once he got it. Just as quickly as the takedown manifested, it evaporated. My sparring partner swiftly escaped, and we were back to our feet. He resumed beating the brakes off me, and all was right in the world again—but that momentary, successful takedown meant I was getting better. I briefly patted myself on the back, but most importantly I got back to work.

Seven

Now, Now, Temper, Temper

My sparring was not limited to multidisciplined sessions. The martial arts class format is usually pretty similar from various style to style. Classes usually follow the format of a warm-up, then a review of what was learned in the last class. After, we would learn a new technique and drill that new technique. Finally would be some form of sparring with an optional cooldown. Not all styles adhere to this specific formula. The Muay Thai class offered at my martial arts academy more often than not left out the sparring component. I assumed sparring was rare in this class because it was a mixed-level class full of beginners, aspiring fighters, and full-fledged professionals. There would be sparring on one fateful night, though.

Our instructor was a national champion. His 18-year-old son, who had been training Muay Thai for what seemed like twice his age, was in this class with me. The instructor's son walked over to me.

"Would you like to spar?" he asked politely.

"Sure, but I am super new to this."

"No worries, I'll go easy."

The bell signifying the beginning of the round rang, and we touched gloves to show one another respect. The sparring started pretty lightly. We traded punches and kicks as if we were taking turns. Before long, our turn-taking approach fell by the wayside, and we exchanged more competitively. Similarly, our light touches had graduated to full-power strikes. A natural progression to assert

16

dominance. This wasn't quite apples to apples though. This kid had been training Muay Thai since before he could walk, and this was my first ever Muay Thai sparring session. He threw perfect striking combinations, up to 10 strikes in quick succession, landing most, if not all of his shots. More frustratingly my return fire was met with his perfect footwork and slick head movements, as such I started to decrease my output. He was scoring at will, and not taking anything off his punches. I couldn't hit the broad side of a barn, but that didn't stop me from throwing each punch I had with bad intentions. Now I'm not sure if it was self-defense, survival, or just being pissed off, but I refused to succumb despite getting lit up like a Christmas tree.

I bit down hard on my mouthpiece and walked through his punches. I backed him up against the padded wall in our gym. One attribute I was blessed with, for better or worse, was the ability to take punishment. I got cracked hard a few times to achieve the positional advantage of backing him up, but once on the inside, I made the fight an ugly fight. If he was able to outclass me with his honed and pretty punches, then I had to take away the space he needed to be so neat and clinical. Once I dictated the range at which we would fight, I was able a land a few punches of my own. When he had had space to work, he had effortlessly ducked, dodged, bobbed, and weaved. Now, he was corralled by the wall I had backed him up against. When you back a fighter into a corner, you ought to be ready to deal with what comes next. What started as light sparring quickly evolved into a live fight. With the intensity of our sparring escalating, our emotions rose to match. We began screaming at one another between blows.

"You punk! Have to back me into the corner to even land a single punch huh?!" our virtuoso fired.

"What's the matter? Can't handle the heat after turning it up?!" I rebutted.

Our yelling got the attention of our coaches. Two of

them ran over and separated us as we continued to bark at one another.

"You better relax, otherwise he'll knock you out," one of the coaches said to me in an effort to calm me down.

"No, he's the one that better calm down! We agreed to spar lightly, and he started teeing off on me! He's lucky I didn't throw him on his head and then snap his arm."

The coach was holding me back, still warning me not to press my luck. He was a bit baffled by my refusal to back down to a seemingly more skilled Thai kickboxer. Our coach (more his really) was blinded by our differing skill levels. He did not see we had unequal fighting spirits, and in this category, it was me with the lion's share. I was aware he was a better striker than me. That honesty with myself provided me the freedom to depart from my current strategy and modality in the middle of sparring in recognition that it wasn't working. Instead, I tapped into where I held the trump cards. I evoked my determination, ingenuity, and tenacity to turn the tide in my favor. My sparring partner and the coach would have preferred that I stay in the domain where my sparring partner was stronger. Sorry, not sorry to spoil the party.

At the end of class, we lined up for our head instructor's closing remarks. After taking care of some housekeeping business, the remainder of his focus was to single me out via a thinly veiled denunciation.

"Some people can't handle sparring. So, maybe we'll have to reserve that for the more seasoned fighters."

Mutually bowing with our instructor signified the end of class. I had to dig deep to find the humility to bow that night.

Eight

With My Tail Tucked

The very next day after my unprofessional and childlike sparring session, I had to go back to my academy to continue training for the fight I had still yet to tell my trainer I had booked. I made sure to get ready early and arrived for the morning session (uncharacteristic of my normal training schedule). I wanted to handle it as maturely as possible, and to me that meant addressing it with the school's owner in person as soon as possible.

I showed up early, before my instructor and academy owner, Brian. I was nervous, but I was ready to apologize. I went in with an open attitude, ready for constructive criticism on how I should have handled the situation differently. Like I said, I was still quite nervous. Brian pulled into the tiny strip-mall usually full of the cars of the martial artists he trains. At this time of the day, it was pretty empty, and he immediately noticed my car in the barren parking lot. After he took some time to make sure he'd gotten all of his equipment together, Brian made his way over towards me.

"What are you doing here so early?" he asked.

"I just couldn't make it tonight, but I still wanted to get my training in," I fabricated.

"Well you're here early for the morning class," Brian informed as he unlocked the door.

"I know, there's actually something I wanted to talk to you about."

"Yeah man, what's up?"

I told him everything that had happened the night before with the national champion Muay Thai kickboxer's son. After laying out my account of what had happened, I apologized for being immature, and for any disrespect I may have shown for Brian and his academy. Respect and honor are tenants in martial arts, and I shamefully was apologizing for my short-sited action. Brian listened to my explanation and apology with patience and a knowing smile that I found a bit unsettling.

"Yeah, I already knew about all that," he confessed.

Of course he would know about any drama happening at his academy—even if he hadn't been there.

"Oh wow, well like I said, I'm really sorry. He asked me to spar. I told him I was inexperienced, and then he started teeing off on me. I don't mean to make any excuses but what was I supposed to do? I am completely open to suggestions here," I asked deferentially.

In between his laughter, Brian spurted out, "Screw that guy, you did exactly the right thing and what I would have had you do."

"Wait, what?" I asked, flabbergasted and relieved all at once.

"His son knew what he was doing, and shouldn't have thrown those punches full force. Sparring is different than fighting."

"Yeah that's what I thought, but I was also in the heat of the moment."

"Don't worry about it, kid."

"OK thanks."

Relief is a funny thing. As soon as I was feeling better about that, my concern of still having to break the news to him of booking a fight without his consultation, much less permission, crept right back in. Aww well, there's plenty of time for that—sort of.

Nine

Zero Confidence

After a couple more weeks of steady training and improving skills, I had worked up enough courage to tell my trainer I had booked that fight behind his back. It was just a matter of picking the time to drop this bomb, gently as I could. After a couple of training sessions passed with the intention to broach the subject and chickening out each time, I decided to man up and just rip the band-aid off. After all, each successive day was getting harder to tell him because it was one day closer to the fight. So, any given "now" was the best time to share the news. One night after BJJ training, I bit the bullet.

I approached my trainer, who was working his star pupil at the time, our gym's only member fighting in the Ultimate Fighting Championship promotion (UFC). I waited for just the right break in the action and for the vibe to calm down. I cleared my throat and piped up.

"Brian, I have something to tell you," I muttered in a deferential tone.

Brian responded in his typical nonchalant way, "What's up man?"

I took a deep breath and cringed my way forward. "I sorta, kinda, booked a fight in Atlantic City." I braced for Brian's inevitable and justified overreaction.

"No sweat man. People get out of those things all the time."

That's it? That's all he had to say?

"Uh Brian, I don't want to get out of it. I want to fight."

"I know man, but there's plenty of time for that. No need to rush it."

"Sorta, but I have this window of time over the summer in between my grad school semesters—"

Brian cut me off. "Dude, you're not ready."

Just then I flashed a sheepish smile and said, "You're right, but I will be."

Brian turned to address our newly signed UFC fighter, Ricardo, looking for back up. Brian asked him to tell me how fighting *really* was. Ricardo obliged even though he didn't really know me that well and did his best to dissuade me.

"Training and fighting are vastly different." Ricardo was a man of few words.

I didn't know how to respond, but the look on my face must have indicated to Ricardo I wasn't convinced.

"Look, a lot of your training goes out the window once you're cracked in the face." He had paraphrased Mike Tyson's "Everyone has a plan till they get punched in the mouth."

Another one of my training partners with fight experience was in the vicinity and contributed a popular saying that floated around the martial arts community. "Every time you're punched in the face, you lose a stripe off your belt."

While I knew they were just looking out for me, it felt to me a lot like they were questioning my masculinity.

"I *know* I can take a punch because I have taken them before."

In as earnest a voice as I've ever heard, Ricardo simply said, "There's a *big* difference from taking a full-on punch and taking a full-on punch from someone who trains."

Ten

Meditation on Getting Cracked in the Face

The time my buddy Chris punched me in the face after the night out for Adam's birthday wasn't the sort of punishment I was citing when defending my ability to take a punch to my trainer and training partners. I love Chris; it's just that his punching technique left something to be desired, nothing against him, he had never trained it. Besides he had much better and more desirable characteristics anyway. One of his best was his ability to get all of us buddies together for a good time, even to this day 20 plus years after we all became friends.

True to form, Chris organized a group of us to go down to his old stomping grounds near Delaware University just a year after we all had graduated college. There was a decent mix of guys and girls, and for once Chris actually delivered on his promise of "thirty definites" he had procured for us all to party together with. Being in our early twenties, it was still a pretty carefree time in our lives despite dipping our toes into the real world. At that age, we all still clung to our self-perceived invincibility, only amplified by being around one another. That said, we were a pretty naïve and happy-go-lucky group, never looking to start any trouble. It was fun to bar hop with a group that big, and when last call was announced, we were all too happy to graduate to greasy late-night food from alcohol.

We were led on a march from the bars to the diner by none other than Chris. Most of us were pretty drunk, but like I was saying, we were happy, simply enjoying our time together. I was at the back of the group with my buddy Nick, or more affectionately known as "Pickles." He and I were roughhousing a bit, but all in good fun. Just then the mood turned super serious. At first it was hard to decipher what was going on because I was still quite drunk. My first thought was that Nick and I were about to get in trouble for our horseplay. As I looked around to assess why the mood got serious, I saw one of the most difficult things I had ever witnessed to this day: my friend Adam lying on the ground as five monsters were kicking his lifeless body.

It took me a moment to comprehend what I was seeing through my inebriation. The image was as jarringly disturbing as it was alien. Once the reality seeped through my drunkenness, it shook me to my core. Those ogres were on their way to killing someone I loved. As drunk as I was, a sobering sight like that had a way of settling priorities really quickly, even if my motor skills were lagging behind. With my newfound understanding of what was happening, I engaged.

"HEY!" I shouted at the top of my lungs. Admittedly crude, yet effective.

What happened next is difficult to convey through the written word. In response to my shouting, all five of the brutes, in perfect synchronicity, transferred their singular focus from violently kicking Adam to me. It was as if a pack of wolves was tearing apart a carcass and a fawn unwittingly stumbled across their path, snapping a tree branch and causing the savage beasts to fixate on something entirely more enticing. I'm not sure if it was their perfectly synched movement, resembling a creepy synchronized swimming team or if it was the look of bloodlust in their eyes, but either way I had never been more scared in my life. Is it odd that a Nelson Mandela quote ran through my mind and actually helped to steel me for what was to come?

"I learned that courage was not the absence of fear, but the triumph over it. The brave man is not he who does not feel afraid, but he who conquers that fear."

Allow me to backtrack just a bit before entering the ensuing melee with you, just to color in the context a little more fully. Unbeknownst to me and only explained after the altercation, was that there was an ongoing culture clash in the parts of Newark, Delaware surrounding the university. The clash was between college students and the similarly aged residents who do not attend college. From the perspective of working-class young adults, the college kids were snobby, entitled, elitists that needed to be brought down a peg or two. From the college students' perspective, their non-college going contemporaries were uncouth, red-necked townies, and were to be regarded as less. Needless to say, the two groups did not particularly like one another, and when alcohol was added into the mix—it served to add more ammunition to the pissing contest (both figuratively and literally). The majority of our group was oblivious to this, as most of us didn't attend Delaware University. The dynamic was more of a minefield than anything else, and Adam was the unlucky one to step on the mine on our way to the diner. On our path, we passed a high retaining wall bordering the sidewalk where those five animals sat looking for trouble. Our group did not have a monopoly on the idea of late night food after drinking, and there were many people making a similar march to satisfy drunken hunger. As people would pass the retaining wall, those hyenas would bark, heckle, bully, and harass anyone and everyone in the hopes they would engage. Then they'd have a reason to take out their existential frustration on some punk yuppie. Most passersby were all too familiar with the dynamic and knew to ignore them. Credit Adam's natural absentminded innocence combined with his blood alcohol level and simply being at the wrong place at the wrong time—and voila, a perfect storm. As it was explained to me afterward, these troublemakers were barking as Adam passed, saying something to effect of:

"Hey! What's your problem?!"

Whereas Adam may have heard it as, "Hey, are you having a problem?" so responded with, "No problem here, why?"

But the hyenas took it as, "What's *your* problem?!"

This was all it took to prompt them to jump off the retaining wall and surround Adam.

"Do something yuppie!" one of them shouted in Adam's face.

To Adam's credit, he wasn't going to simply just take that abuse despite his obvious disadvantage. "Screw you, loser," he said matter-of-factly, as he attempted to walk past them.

Well, that's all they needed to assault Adam. One of the five sucker-punched Adam from behind, dropping him to the ground, and as you know by now, that wasn't enough for them as they all began to savagely kick him.

Fast forward back to my stumbling across this scene and yelling out, "HEY!" The animals looked up at their new target. As they slowly walked over to me, licking their chops, I remember having the distinct thought, *Well you always wanted to know how you'd fair in a fight*. My curiosity had always been in a *fair* fight though.

A quick reminder of my stature for perspective: I am 5'8" tall and at the time was walking around at about 170 lbs. Thanks to my wrestling experience spanning back to when I had been 13-years-old, I was hyper-sensitive to the heights and weights of opponents—and that sense graces me to this day. Of the five animals, I put the *smallest* one at 5'10" and 200 lbs. I estimated the largest to be about 6'4", weighing about 260 lbs., with the rest of the guys slotting in between. Oh, and they were all built like solid athletes—think football player types. *Whoo-boy! This is going to be rough.*

At this stage of my life, my martial arts training consisted of high school wrestling, about one year of karate, and about three months of Brazilian Jiu-Jitsu.

The trouble with the wrestling and BJJ is they are primarily ground fighting arts, and after seeing what those guys were doing to Adam on the ground, I thought my best strategy would be to keep this on our feet as long as possible. Instinctively I took to a fighting stance—my karate fighting stance—as they all circled me.

When fighting multiple men, you should keep as many of them in front of you as possible. I was facing five, which meant keeping three of them in front of me and leaving the remaining two the benefit of moving undetected. While fighting the three men in front of me, one of the two behind me would approach uncontested and crack me in the back of the head.

There is a reason why in sanctioned fights blows to the back of the head are illegal, and it has to do with being an easier spot to disrupt someone's equilibrium. So, with unchecked freedom to swing their overly massive fists as hard as they could, they hit their mark. When they connected with the back of my head, I would suffer a momentary lapse in my consciousness and my body would "turn off," causing me to drop to the ground. This was where I learned that I was blessed with a quick recovery time—truly nothing I can take credit for. While I was careening to the ground was when my consciousness returned. Luckily, I had the situational awareness to know that taking a moment or two to collect myself was not in the cards. For if I were to take that moment, those animals would have capitalized in the same way they were kicking my friend. With that awareness, I simply popped up and kept fighting the three that were in front of me. After throwing a few punches, I was inevitably met with another blindsided strike to the back of my head. This cycle repeated itself a few more times. I'd fight what was in front of me, get clocked by what was behind me, momentarily lose consciousness, come to, pop up, and begin again.

After what felt like an eternity, but was probably only about a minute or less, these savages must have thought this guy they were beating up was one crazy son of a bitch because he just wouldn't stay down. That, or perhaps they just got bored or tired of kicking the crap out of me.

Either way, they all ran off. Now I was spared the fate Adam suffered by being able to get to my feet each time I was knocked down, but I was most certainly worse for the ware. I felt banged up, but I knew that I was not seriously injured. I also knew I had just decisively taken a one-way beating. After dusting myself off, I was about to try and find Adam and tend to him. Just then, Pickles ran out beyond me, chasing after my assaulters while screaming at the top of his lungs,

"HEY YOU PUSSY MOTHERFUCKERS, WHERE ARE YOU GOING?!"

I was in complete and utter disbelief watching my friend run out ahead of me to taunt my and Adam's attackers when he had been nowhere to be found when Adam was beaten down and when I took my own beating. Funny thing about being called a "pussy motherfucker": it tends to get your attention, especially for thugs like these. The delinquents were about a hundred meters away when Pickles called out his insult. Three of the five attackers pulled an about face and started charging Nick, who had run out beyond me to be sure his insult was heard. Now despite being dumbfounded and very cross with Nick for his untimely bravery, these monsters were bearing down on him. If those monsters were able to deliver me the worst beating of my life to that point, I thought that they would kill him. And even though Pickles did deserve something between a stern talking to and a slap upside the head as far as I could tell, that would have to wait because his life was being threatened.

Those three thugs were now running full speed, bee-lining it straight for Pickles. My only option was to enter into a sprint myself to get between Pickles and the three returning hooligans. I'm not sure where I found the energy after fighting five overgrown men to then sprint, in which the finish line was another fight—this time outnumbered three to one. I didn't think it would be easy, but fighting three savages had to be easier than fighting five of them. I was crucially aware that numbers mattered and not only was it two less this time, they were in staggered starting positions when they turned to run back. Effectively, this meant for all intents and purposes they were coming in one at a time. And you better believe for damn sure that if I was ok with my initial odds at five to one, I was happy to improve to three to one. Better than that, I realized I would briefly have a one-on-one fight with that first guy. We were running full-tilt at one another, and I was experiencing a mix of emotions between euphoria and fear. I knew full well that my odds would diminish drastically over time as each thug caught up to the fray. With this realization, I understood I would have to knock the first punk out cold, enabling a two-on-one fight. We were two speeding trains on a collision course. I began to cock my punch while sprinting, getting ready to unleash and convert all of my combined potential force of mass and speed to kinetic force by delivering my punch right to this scumbag's face. I envisioned taking his head clean off. I had made my mind up; this time I was no longer the victim. It was my turn to be the savage.

Focused on the task at hand, time slowed and my senses heightened. I felt the soft earth under my feet give way as I pushed hard with each step towards the anarchy I was to initiate this time. My fist closing in on its target with the full lock of a heat-seeking missile, I got a glimpse of my adversary's face. Ordinarily I might have felt human again, and held back some of my malintent, but I was in full-on protection mode and after what this son of a bitch did to my dear friend, I was more than ready to learn what was in the darkest depths of my soul and unchain that dark beast for protective right action.

I was an atom being sped up to near lightspeed in a particle accelerator, and my adversary was no different. Our paths were destined for a collision of epic proportions...or so I had thought.

What I didn't know when my buddy Pickles called out,

"Hey you pussy motherfuckers, where are you going?" was that he was already on the phone with the police and was instructed to keep the attackers there by any means necessary as the police were only a couple blocks away. I couldn't know it in the moment, but whereas Pickles' call out seemed beyond believably dumb, it turned out to be genius. The cops arrived at the exact moment before my reengagement with the enemy. Those cops were quite a force on to themselves, arriving with between 15 and 20 squad cars. Adding that into the mix of an already chaotic situation made a crazed situation more volatile. The police quickly seized control of the mayhem.

All the police knew was that a group of people were being attacked by another group of people, so when they arrived, I still had rage in my heart and daggers for eyes primed for the next skirmish. Not the best look to have when meeting a throng of police officers. The first order of business for the newly established authority to this shindig was to sort combatants and noncombatants. As a combatant, I was rounded up indiscriminatingly with the three of the five thugs that returned to reengage.

The police separated the thugs and I from the onlookers by placing myself and those assholes on that high retaining wall right next to one another. As my heart rate returned to normal and the sobering effect of the preceding events set in, a calm washed over me, knowing my friends were no longer in danger. In my newly found calmness, there was still chaos all around. As the 30 plus police officers were sorting out what had happened, the women of our group did their best to testify on my behalf. They all took turns running up to the police, one notch below hysterical screaming, as they pointed right at me.

"He's the hero! He's the one that saved all of us!"

Despite their testimonials contributing to the chaos, 15 women all screaming the same thing tends to have an effect on the understanding of the precession of events. I must also confess, having 15 women all screaming that you're a hero has an effect on a guy. Feeling bolstered and emboldened by my adoring "fans," I decided to give into my immature urge and gloated in front of the three punks. I looked over to them with a cocky gleam in my eye, and once I knew I had their undivided attention, I blew them a few quick kisses in short succession, as it was the most demeaning thing I could think of. Without skipping a beat, they reacted by getting up, making their way over to me to recommence our unfair fight. I couldn't believe it. There was a freaking army of police officers surrounding us. Realizing that the police might not be able to protect me in time despite their numbers, I found myself gearing up for that next round of our fight. Just as we were to entangle again, the nearest police officer only about five feet away, nonchalantly turned around and said but a single word.

"Really?"

Thankfully that's all it took for them to tuck their tails and put them back in their place. Tempting fate, I flashed them a wink and a shit-eating grin.

Meanwhile, Adam was being attended to by paramedics in an ambulance on the way to the hospital. He ended up with over 20 stitches in his head and face, with swelling and bruising that had him unrecognizable. Thankfully, he made a total recovery and looks as good as he ever did! A couple of months later, Brad and Adam went back down to Delaware to offer testimony of the happenings on that fateful night. Disappointingly despite Brad and Adam's best effort, those delinquents only received a slap on the wrist. Their biggest take away came as a result of their sober impressions of the three offenders, best represented in a single sentence they had for me upon their return.

"Damn, those guys were big."

"You don't say!" I laughed.

Eleven

Auxiliary Support

After letting in my trainer on my booking and intention to fight, he ratcheted up the intensity of my training. He started circling in the professional fighters into my rotation with increased frequency. He took my training wheels off by instructing my pro sparring partners to really put it on me. As it turns out, my sneaking suspicion that they were taking it easy on me previously was then confirmed. After that, having the snot kicked out of me became something of a regular occurrence. I've heard of growing pains, but this took it to a new level.

Our trainer had taken the reigns off our stable of beasts. For the first time, I got a firsthand account of Ricardo's foreboding that there was a difference in a trained fighter's punch compared to that of a street thug's. Even sparring with full 16-oz gloves (MMA gloves are only 4 oz) I would be dropped by punches. I guess this was to be expected. What took me by surprise was getting dropped by single shots to the body. It was some feeling to be temporarily paralyzed by a single heavily padded punch. "Experience: that most brutal of teachers. But you learn, my God do you learn," said William Nicholson. And learn I did. Slowly but surely acquiring all those lumps led to learning how to receive less of them.

All the while through my training, I was also working on the back-end of stuff. Dealing with the fight promoter, Scott, was one hell of an experience. Talk about eccentric (and I would come to learn later that his look matched his personality). Gregarious doesn't come close to describing his verbosity. Tickets had to be bought directly through him, and when my supporters purchased their tickets, he would keep each one of them on the phone for half an hour or more talking about me. Every one of my supporters commented on the eccentricity of Scott and Scott's apparent affinity towards me despite never having met me. Oh well, it's better to be liked than disliked I suppose. I was fortunate to have so many supporters that it actually changed my position on the fight card. Originally, being a no-name fighter, I was placed early on the card, the prelims if you will. But, because I had about a hundred supporters buy tickets for a 1,400-seat theater, the promoter was worried about a mass exodus early in his show. As a result of having so many supporters willing to endure Scott's loquaciousness, it was as if my supporters had hoisted me into the desirable position later on the fight card. I am fortunate to have received much support from many people over the course of my many trials. I am eternally grateful for all the support from the people in my life. I may be most in debt to those supporters who endured hour-long conversations Scott cornered them into.

Twelve

Engage the Cynics

So, my training schedule and diet back then doesn't seem as crazy as I remember it. Maybe that's just it—all those years help to fade the pain and work that went into it all. Anyway, here it is:

9 a.m.: coffee and granola
10 a.m.: 5-mile run or hill sprints; protein shake
11 a.m.: breakfast—1% milk fat cottage cheese with bananas mixed in, with more coffee
2 p.m.: lunch—2 chicken salad sandwiches from Wegmans with organic chocolate milk
5 p.m.: commute to go train

6 p.m.: Jiu-Jitsu

8 p.m.: Muay Thai or MMA sparring

9:30 p.m.: commute home; protein shake

10:30 p.m.: shower, ice my body; dinner (lean protein, veggies, small portion of a starch)

12 a.m.: Bed

Like I said, looking back on all that, it doesn't even feel like it was a lot. But I can tell you this: it was so much in fact that even though I was scheduled to take two online courses for grad school that summer, I barely finished the first. After struggling through the first class, I went rogue and decided on my own that I would not take the second one. I decided I would find a way to make it up during the next academic year. A necessary evil that would still come back to bite me later on. That said, I don't do well with multitasking and given that I was scheduled to be locked in a cage with a man training to kill me, it wasn't too difficult to set the fight as my top priority. After my fight, I would get to whatever else needed tending to. Despite looking over that seemingly sparse schedule, I do know it took everything out of me. A quick word on what might be missing from the schedule—lifting and all of the other martial arts I had previously studied (wreslting, boxing, judo, karate, etc.) Firstly, there is for sure some crossover in those skills. Secondly, there are only so many hours in a week. Lastly Jiu-Jitsu and Muay Thai comprise two of the major three components of an MMA fight (wrestling being the third base of MMA).

I had the most training in wrestling to date, so I figured it best to train my weaker skill sets. The reason that I chose endurance training (running and sprinting) over lifting is twofold: I've always been naturally strong, especially for my weight, and my endurance has always had to be something I needed to work on. Again, I decided to work on my weaknesses. Also, the idea of becoming exhausted in the fight with a fresh opponent in front of me was my nightmare scenario.

One night after coming home from a long and hard sparring session where I had been exposed to the "shark tank" (One fighter stays on the mat as other fresh fighters are circled in round by round), I limped into my cousin Eric's house. He asked me how I did and how I was feeling, and I shot him a look like I would be needing an extra-long shower and icing session that night. After said shower and taping bags of ice to every inch of my body, I checked my email. Low and behold my promoter had provided me with my opponent, now just a few short weeks out from my fight. He was a Muay Thai fighter, and I was able to track him down on Facebook. His profile picture was from one of his bouts. He was shredded, tall, long, and lean. Instantaneously I started putting a game plan together on how I would beat this archetypal fighter. Peering over my shoulder, my cousin was spying on what I had discovered. He laughed a nervous laugh.

"Dude, he's ripped and looks like one tough dude."

"Not as tough as me," I fired back with no real way of knowing.

"What happens if you lose?"

"I won't."

"How can you be so sure?"

"Because I know how hard I'm training and I know what I'm capable of."

"What if your opponent is saying the same thing? That he won't lose because he knows how hard he's working and what he's capable of?"

"Simple. He'd be wrong."

Eric walked off with dismissive body language and confidently postulated, "I know what's going to happen."

"Oh you do, do you? Do tell."

"You're not going to fight."

"Excuse me?! You think I'm going to chicken out?!"

He pondered for a moment and declared, "Not exactly, but you'll get some injury that'll enable you to save face and back out of the fight."

His smugness and confidence in his statement ticked me off. "I thought you knew me, man. Not only will I answer the bell for this fight, I will one hundred percent guarantee I'll win it."

"You're being ridiculous. You can't know that. Besides, it won't be your fault; everyone will understand you can't fight if you're injured. Look at you now. You're covered from head to toe in ice. The training alone is breaking you down. You cannot sustain this. Even if you don't quit, your body will—it'll be your perfect way out."

"Wow you really don't know me at all. Thanks for wishing an injury on me. Thanks for the lack of confidence in my abilities. Understand this: Should I suffer an injury, not only will I fight injured, I will win injured."

"You'll see. Don't sweat it though. You'll be able to save face."

"No, it is you that will see. *When* I win, you'll have to eat the crow for doubting me."

We don't get to choose how our inspiration comes. I much prefer the variety of proving my supporters right than proving the naysayers wrong. Choose your corner wisely, roll with the punches, and take it how it comes. As it would turn out, my opponent would get swapped last minute. Instead of the Muay Thai fighter I was originally matched up against making his MMA debut, it would now be a boxer in his second MMA fight. Just another proverbial punch to roll with. Chris Borders lost a close decision in his first fight but showcased dynamite for hands. I figured I would have the edge in the grappling department, but I was more keen for the opportunity to test my own hands—and chin I would come to find.

Thirteen

Sticky Situation

If one sticks with something long enough, one cannot help but get better. I kept to my minimalist's training schedule day after day. Icing each night became my healing elixir; it allowed me to get up the next day and do it all again. It wasn't until I signed up for my fight that I had consistently sparred MMA in my life. In the relatively short time I allotted myself to train for this fight, I began to make huge strides. When I was at the beginning of my training camp journey, I was getting beat up every minute of every round. After having the bulk of the training behind me and with just a couple of weeks before my fight, my sparring sessions began to look and feel a little different. I mean, I still lost most of the time, but I was not discouraged for a few reasons:

1. My beatings were at the hands of professional fighters, and I would be facing an amateur.

2. Despite being the nail more often than the hammer, I had my moments—I started to win about 40% of the time.

3. If nothing else, I learned I could endure months on end of sustained beatings from professional fighters.

All that is something, right?

Consistency of practice is more than half the battle. "I fear not the man who has practiced 10,000 kicks once, but I fear the man who has practiced one kick 10,000 times," wise words from none other than the late great Bruce Lee. That said, as martial artists, we will forever learn and then attempt new techniques to fold into our arsenals. Our martial arts academy brought in a top BJJ black belt to teach us a wrinkle in his game via his traveling seminar. I definitely learned some new techniques, setups, and approaches in his seminar. I would rank the level of intensity when it comes to training in order of most intense to least intense:

1. MMA sparring
2. Muay Thai sparring
3. Jiu-Jitsu sparring (or rolling)
4. Drilling (practicing) techniques

Please do not mistake this for being in order of importance. Drilling is the least sexy of the lot, but most martial artists will tell you it is way more important than sparring. I only bring the intensity distinction to set the scene. Drilling is not a competitive act, but rather a cooperative one. It is akin to learning a choreography so that later one can call on it through muscle memory and use it improvisationally in intense moments, under the bright lights or in a dark alley.

Due to this class being a seminar, we had affiliated schools in on our class, and I got partnered with someone around my size from our affiliate school. What he maybe lacked in years of training, he made up for with respect and reverence for learning the craft. Drilling each one of the new techniques, he and I began to find a flow and worked well together. We were towards the end of the seminar with one more technique to learn (a deep half-guard technique). We began to get a feel for this new technique. We kept drilling and then our guest instructor asked us all to finish one last rep before coming to the center of the mat for some final thoughts. It was my partner's turn, and as luck would have it, as he executed the final repetition of the last technique, he lost control of his body and slammed his knee directly into the ridge of my eyebrow. It didn't feel particularly good, but martial arts isn't tiddlywinks, and sometimes you take the odd inadvertent blow. You don't join swim team not expecting to get wet. Same goes for martial arts: you will take your lumps. Thinking nothing of getting my bell rung, as it has happened before more than enough times, I shook out the cobwebs and started over towards the center of the mat for our guest instructor's final thoughts. As I was making my way over, my trainer came racing over.

"Dude, you gotta go clean yourself off!"

"What do you mea—"

Before I could finish my sentence, what I thought was sweat started to splatter on the ground around me. Upon closer inspection it was red, and last I had checked I didn't sweat red. Turns out that incidental knee to my dome opened up a one-inch-long and half-inch-wide gash directly above my eye. Only the worst location for a cut because blood could flow unobstructed into my eye if it were reopened. I knew this cut jeopardized my clearance to fight, as my fight was only two weeks away. Almost worse, my first thought was that this happening could make my cousin's foreboding jinx come to fruition.

As I was turning an entire roll of paper towels crimson, I overheard from the bathroom what our guest instructor was imparting.

"I encourage everyone to go out and compete. There are sides of ourselves that are buried and only revealed in stressful situations, outside of our comfort bubbles. When you compete, one of two things can happen—you could win or you could lo—earn."

Essentially by merely competing, we had an opportunity to gain.

Once I got the gash to stop spurting, I was able to use gauze and a bunch of tape to control the rest of the bleeding. On my drive home, I managed to keep my freaking out at only the level of a simmer. I stopped at a pharmacy to pick up butterfly bandages and super glue. I heard somewhere along the way that superglue would work for cuts. Not smart—I'm sure my doctor dad wouldn't be so proud. With wound care in tow, I made my way back home to my cousin's. I was dreading the inevitable, "I told you so." There was no hiding the wound as I walked through the door. I was met with Ellen's, my cousin's wife, gasp. The gasp caught my cousin's attention, and he came to see what all the commotion was about. He expressed concern, but I was skeptical. To his credit, he didn't *say*, "I told you so." But, it seemed to me that he was thinking it.

"So, what are you going to do?"

"I'm going to glue this thing shut, heal, and win my fight in a couple of weeks' time."

"You only have two weeks. That isn't enough time for a cut that deep and wide to heal. There's no shame in pulling out because of this freak accident."

"It will heal, and I will win my fight," I said over my shoulder as I walked off to go tend my wound.

I couldn't get the superglue to hold the gash closed. Disclaimer: Don't try what I tried at home—seek immediate medical attention should something similar happen to you. Thankfully, I was able to get the butterfly bandages to hold it closed. Then I superglued over the top of it, because YOLO, as the kids say.

Fourteen

Shark Tank from Hell

Fight week is for staying loose and hungry. Rolling light was perfect as to minimize the odds of reopening my gash. As a precaution, I still taped my head before each training session with about a 1/3 of a roll of tape. Picture old-timey civil war wounded. Best laid plans, right? My trainer mustn't have gotten the memo. In my last day of training before I was to head down to Atlantic City, he wanted to see where I was at. He wanted to know if I was ready. He lined up the most challenging shark tank session through all of my fight training to date.

Maybe it was my inexperience, or maybe it was my machismo—not wanting to appear weak in front of my trainer, my team, myself. So, I didn't question, complain, or balk. I bit down on my mouthpiece and battled one last time before I went to war. Ordinarily, a shark tank session would be between three to five guys, sometimes re-rotating some of my sparring partners back in. However, this time my trainer set me up with seven men for seven rounds. The addition of two rounds doesn't sound like that much more. As an amateur fighter, I was only preparing for three rounds at three minutes each with a one-minute break between rounds. So, what's an extra six minutes really? I had gotten used to going 15 minutes, could 21 really be that much harder? Yes. A thousand times yes.

You see, going full-tilt with every muscle group, with injury as a penalty if you let your guard down even for a moment, causes a fatigue like nothing else. Mercifully my trainer kept those seven rounds at the three-minute duration. Sadistically though, he only gave me a 45-second break between the rounds before a fresh guy would cycle in. Be it that it was so late in the training camp, at this stage we were only wrestling and grappling.

Even if I didn't have the gash over my eye, I seriously doubt my trainer would have had us full-on sparring. Even still, it was enough. Mind you, I was absolutely in the best shape of my life. I was ready for what was to come, or at least I told myself that. The first few rounds I was cleaning up shop—dominating the wrestling exchanges and pulling off at least one submission per round. You guessed it, as the rounds went on, the proficiency and skill of my training partners increased.

By round three, I was the one in survival mode, getting taken down at will and fighting submission attempt after submission attempt. Round four brought more of the same. I found myself desperately trying to actively recover as my training partners were trying to rip my limbs from their home. Through rounds five and six I was no longer able to hold my defenses, and I began to get submitted.

We would restart, and I would get tapped again and again. The whole gym of about 40 onlookers was cheering me on, shouting whatever encouraging thing they could to help me get through this hell.

When the bell rang for round seven, I was definitively the most exhausted I had ever been. I began to question the shape I was in. I began to question if I was ready for my fight. I even questioned the competency of my trainer for subjecting me to this so close to the fight, both from a physical standpoint and a mental one as well. Exhausted to the point of near collapse, my trainer cycled in a weaker training partner, one I was accustomed to being head and shoulders better than.

There was a glimmer of hope that arose in me, believing I could get through this round with *this* training partner. However, in the state of being totally spent, this sparring partner I had been accustomed to beating handily started to beat me—badly. He was submitting me. All of my efforts were summoned to defense, and it didn't matter, I couldn't stop his onslaught.

After taking my beating for the duration of the round, I heard the 10-second indicator for the end of the round go off. I thought to myself, *Almost there. I can get through this.* Just then, my trainer announced that I was not done until I escaped on my own. He instructed my partner to fight through the bell and to not let up because that would not serve me in my fight. He did as he was instructed. This last round went on for almost double all the others.

Thankfully though, no fresh guy was circled in. That in conjunction with me finally finding my second wind enabled me to muster all of the little strength I had left for one definite and concerted, explosive effort. I was able to sweep (reverse) my partner and found myself in a dominant position. The crowd of martial arts students erupted into cheers, and I collapsed thinking I might die.

No exaggeration, it took me close to an hour for me to fully catch my breath. My predominant thought immediately after was, *That was stupid. That completely depleted my gas tank—even my reserve tank. This is too close to my fight. Oh well, can't go back now—what's done is done.*

You know the staples "easy button"? After that, I wanted to push a corollary stupid button for the robotic voice to exclaim, "That was stupid."

Fifteen

Ball is in the Air

Well, the training was complete. What was done was done, and what would be would be. The phrase, "The ball is in the air," comes from golf. Once the golfer goes through the entire mechanism of his swing (head still, proper backswing, straight front arm, good follow through, etc.), it all leads to making contact with the golf ball. Once the swing is complete, there is nothing more the golfer can do to affect the ball's trajectory or resting place. The phrase really means the work is done. It may have been a perfect swing, placing the ball on a seemingly perfect trajectory, but upon its landing, it took a funny hop and got kicked into a sand trap or water hazard. The opposite could happen as well. The golfer may have taken the worst, least fundamentally sound swing, sending the ball careening into the woods, and yet it bounced off a tree, landing the ball smack in the middle of the fairway, green, or even in the cup. Those scenarios depict a lucky knockout punch landing. Point is, there is little if anything to be gained by placing one's focus on how the ball may bounce. Smart money dictates you focus on your swing (or really things we have control over).

I felt really good about my training. I was undoubtedly in the best shape of my life. I was well prepared and paid my dues with blood, sweat, and tears. I was forged in the fire of sparring professional fighters. I was ready. I hoped.

Sixteen

Learn and Do It Better

The training may have been done, but I still had one looming responsibility that no fighter looked forward to—the dreaded weight cut. My natural, walking-around weight when I'm not working out too consistently is around 185 lbs. Given that I'm merely 5'8", I believe that might put me close to obesity on a body mass index (BMI) chart. Thankfully I carry more muscle than the average bear, but I'm nothing to write home about at my out-of-shape walking weight. In my personal training days, I got up to about 200 lbs., and was definitely beefier, but I wasn't exactly cut or ripped as I still carried some fat. With all the running and fight training (effectively more cardio), I was at the trimmest and lightest I had been since my freshman year of high school, where I went from football season directly into wrestling season. The best measure I had for my fitness was the six pack I had earned for the first time in my life and only time since. While from a vanity standpoint I sure was happy about it, it had a deeper meaning—that I was at the lowest body fat I had ever been. I never had it measured, but I'd estimate it to be between 4-8%. That is to say, I did not have much excess weight to lose, and I was walking around at about 170 lbs. The weight class in which I was fighting was super welterweight with a 154 lbs. weight limit. As a former high school wrestler, I had had some experience with shedding those excess pounds, but I never learned how to do it properly. This time around, I had more respect for the process and would shed the weight over a longer period of time. The most weight I had lost during high school wrestling was 10 lbs. in four hours. Obviously not healthy in the least. I had been reminded of my moronic actions by my parents as I had been losing the weight. I would put on three to four pairs of sweatpants and sweatshirts and run up and down our stairs, periodically dotted with stepping into the bathroom that I had turned into a makeshift steam room by running the shower on its hottest setting without ventilating any of it. My parents would switch between yelling at me for ruining my kidneys for loosing so much water weight in too short of period of time, and yelling at me for warping the door and doorframe by running the shower the way I had been. Of course, they had been right, but adolescence has a built-in function to help one ignore their parents' good advice (even if they were say, a doctor and a nurse as mine were).

At least, as a man in my mid-twenties, I now knew to give myself more time and to take the weight off gradually. So instead of 10 lbs. in four hours, it would be 16 lbs. in 48 hours.

Strangely, I prepared to starve and dehydrate myself before the most physically demanding task I had ever asked of my body by shopping for nutritious food and drink. Really it was just one more way of being prepared— one more way of focusing on what I could control in the midst of the chaos I was about to enter, taking advantage of any small opportunity to stack the odds in my favor. If I had to put my body through this torture session before I were to engage in combat, I wanted to refuel it the best way I could after the fact. What this meant was complex carbohydrates, lean proteins, and plenty of electrolytes. I don't need to tell you that being around such a bounty of mana was not so easy while I was quite literally starving myself to make weight. A necessary evil worth suffering for.

Now for the deed of taking off those pounds. While the method of sweating off the pounds may have evolved from sweating in my parents' humid bathroom, the fundamental process was the same, I just used upgraded facilities. My local gym had a sauna, steam room, and hot tub for me to shed the weight. I began the Wednesday before my Friday night fight. Marginally better than a few hours beforehand on Friday, wouldn't you say? I'm not sure how it came to be, but I had an unusual weight cutting music mix that had evolved over the years. It consisted of some Dave Matthews, Goo Goo Dolls, and Jethro Tull. Again, I am unsure as to why those artists gave me the strength to push through—helping me to tough out five more minutes in a sauna at a time—but it most certainly did.

Seventeen

Atlantic City or Bust

With the ball in the air, all that was left to do was pack my bags. One bag to be packed would contain all of my clothes and toiletries, another would contain all of my fight gear—shorts, gloves, mouthpiece, shin guards, and groin protector. And one more bag full of the modern-day mana to restore my depleted body after the weight cut: sports drinks, electrolyte water, protein bars, and the such.

With bags packed, it was time to say my goodbyes to my cousin and his family. I was to make this journey on my own. There was serious concern in the expressions of all my extended family as I said my goodbyes—hugging me extra tight as they implored me to be safe. Those hugs betrayed their lacking confidence in me. I did my best to reassure them (or maybe it was myself I was reassuring). "Fear not, I will return victorious." Truth is though, I was resigned and committed to return "with my shield or on it."

With goodbyes said, hugs given, car packed and fueled,

I set off for Atlantic City, heading off in my 1999 Mazda. It reminded me of my last trip down with my best buddy John to play poker. On that trip, we had found ourselves involved in a high-speed car pursuit in speeds of excess of 140 mph, and had encountered a raging road goer as we had hit traffic and a merge.

As we were exiting the garden state parkway, on to the Atlantic City Expressway, traffic had slowed to a stop. People were trying to cut the line of cars by illegally using the shoulder. When one such motorist tried to cut ahead of me in the same way, I, perhaps immaturely, decided to draw a line in the sand, disallowing him from unfairly getting in front. We wound up being side by side with his shoulder cutting in, preventing him from maneuvering around to get ahead. We locked eyes, and without skipping a beat he yelled at me, "You drive a gay man's car." He was driving some sort of German Sedan, a status symbol of an automobile. There indeed is a stereotype of Mazda Miata's being an effeminate vehicle. Aware of this, I didn't care so much for the dual reason of the handling characteristics of the car (appealing to the auto enthusiast in me), and I got a great deal on it. However, I did care on some level, evidenced by going out of my way to adorn my license plates with covers similar to the ones that say, "I'd rather be fishing." Mine said at the top, "I'd rather be…choking you out." And at the bottom, "Jiu-Jitsu fighter." I had got it at a tournament as a giveaway and hadn't won anything else at that tournament. That's ok, those plate covers have given me more use than any medal or trophy I've ever earned. So, when he called me out for driving a gay man's car, I retorted, "Oh yeah read the license plates on this so-called gay man's car." Now, I'm not gay, but that's immaterial because my sexual orientation doesn't define me or anyone else. And this asshole deserved to be choked out by a gay man since he was using the term pejoratively. I directed his attention to the adorned message on my license plate since he had a perfect view now that he was stuck behind me.

After winning that most important challenge of my life, I could gleefully bask in my victory for the rest of time. Oh wait, what's that—it was silly? It wasn't worth it? There would be unforeseen consequences for such silly actions? Well what were they? Once the merge was behind us, and we entered the Atlantic City Expressway, the traffic opened up. With the newly found automotive freedom, our friend in the German Sedan decided to exact his revenge. You see, John and I were in need of refueling, and there was a gas station in the middle of the Atlantic City Expressway, reached only by a rare left exit. Just as we were exiting to gas up before the last leg into Atlantic City, our friend sped ahead of us and hurled a full beer can out of his window at us. Well, he must have had some experience with hurling beer out of moving vehicles because this guy shot a perfect bulls-eye—a direct hit on the windshield. Sustaining an impact from a full beer at highway speed was startling and frightening enough. Having it explode and blind you as you are in the middle of maneuvering to exit the highway while closing in on a concrete divider was downright terrifying. With scant moments to react, I engaged the windshield wipers, revealing we were just a second or two from impacting the concrete barrier. "Holy shit!" John shouted. I initiated an input to swerve and avoided the barrier. Only it was a bit of an over-correction, causing the car to fish tale, and the rear began to overtake the front of the car. Thankfully, I had some experience hooning a car in my youth and would initiate such skids regularly. I learned how to counter-steer in the direction of the skid, which was counterintuitive. I caught the car and regained control just in time from spinning and hurtling into the gas station pumps—which would have done more than tickle. I asked John, "Are you ok?"

"Yeah, what the hell though?"

"Should I catch him and get his license plate for us to

give to the cops?"

"Go for it!"

Now with the gas station being situated in between the opposite direction of the flow of traffic meant that there were no curves to the exit ramp or on-ramp. So, I was simply able to drop a gear, mash the throttle, and take the on-ramp back onto the highway, much to our assaulter's utter disbelief. He instantly took off. John, without skipping a beat, pulled out his phone and called 9-1-1. As John was getting the police dispatch on the line, I was in hot pursuit of this asshole. Full disclaimer that this was not our smartest decision, but when someone threatens your life in that way, adrenaline has a way of taking over. His German Sedan had about 400 hp, and I was only working with about 140 hp. But, my car was lighter, and I had track-driving experience under my belt in addition to my high school hooligan ways. Our villain tried to extract every horse out of his 260-horse advantage as we were careening towards Atlantic City itself. Looking at the speedometer, I saw 80, 90, 100 mph indicated. "We are traveling eastbound on the Atlantic City Expressway in pursuit of a man who threw an entire beer out of his vehicle at highway speed, and it exploded on our windshield. We are pursuing in order to provide you his license plate number." Now we had reached 110, 120, 130 mph. "Our guy isn't slowing down. He's not getting away though." At 140 mph, a little bit of sense crept into this creep's head—he realized he was not going to be able to shake me and began to slow down to a reasonable highway speed again. John was able to relay the license plate number to the police. Just then, a peculiar thing happened—our guy began to slow down below highway speeds to about 40 mph. Instantly my brain spools up to discern why he might do this. The potential for him to harm us by use of firearm jumped the line and received all of my attention. At this point, I started making evasive maneuvers. "What's he doing?"

"I don't know, but I'm not going to stick around to find out either."

Not wanting to worry John that I was worried he was maneuvering to get a clean shot, I simply kept my distance and made sure he never had an unobstructed line of sight to us. The police were still on the line and had given the same directive to maintain a safe distance. The Atlantic City Expressway comes to an end at a stoplight where one can either make a left or a right at the end of the road. I had decided well before we got there that we were simply going to go the opposite way from this punk and leave it to the cops from then on out. The punk turned left; we turned right. I gave the last known heading to the cops and parked in the nearest garage. John and I looked at each other and said simultaneously, "What the hell was that?"

John then asks, "So is that a good omen or a bad one before we go off to gamble?"

I shrugged my shoulders. "Well we're ok, and we got his license plate."

"True, good omen it is."

Turns out lady luck was fickle and disinterested—John won $100, and I lost $100. Though if she had to choose when to impart her luck, I was glad we got it when we did.

Eighteen

Taking Care of Business

We are back to present in my Mazda. I pull into the parking garage of the Tropicana, where I and all of my supporters would be staying. The parking garage was quite a way's away from the hotel check-in counter, and as I loaded up like a pack mule—a dehydrated pack mule—I lamented the mere distance I had to cross with my heavy burden and the remaining weight I still had to lose. I dragged myself to the check-in desk, and then to my room where I could unload my bags. I lay down on the bed to rest my weary dehydrated body. So much to do and so little time. I roused myself to start taking care of business. First thing was first, taking off this weight. Well actually, I needed to first track down a scale to have a proper reference point to link my weight to the scales I was using back home. I put on my bathing suit and went down to the concierge to inquire where I might find a scale. He racked his brain and initially couldn't think if the whole place even had one. Eventually, he said, "I cannot guarantee we have one, but if we do it will probably be at the first-aid station."

"Great, would you mind pointing me in that direction?" Getting lost in the vast casino, I eventually found my way to an off the beaten path nook in the casino—I guessed they tucked this thing away because illness in plain sight didn't facilitate gambling. Anyway, I knocked on the door and was startled by the two nurses at their posts.

"Hi, young man, what seems to be the problem?"

"Oh no problem here. I was told there might be a scale here?"

They looked at me inquisitively. "Son, I think we have a scale in the back, but why on earth do you need to weigh yourself in the middle of the day at a casino? From our eyes, you look mighty fine and ought not to be concerned with your weight." They flashed flirty smiles.

I blushed somewhat easily, and they brought it out. "Thanks, I actually am fighting my first sanctioned fight tomorrow, and I need to check my weight before I go sit in the sauna to see how much weight I take off in a given time at this new sauna."

"Oh, wow. That's a first for us. It seems like you have it down to a science. Sure hun, it's right there in the corner. Help yourself."

"Thanks, I need to be pretty meticulous about it

because if I'm off even by a fraction of a pound, I will be barred from fighting." Still blushing, I continued, "For that reason, I need to strip naked to know exactly what I weigh."

The nurse was wearing glasses and looked out over them as she bit the end of her pen. "That's no problem, go right ahead." I got wide-eyed and blushed a few more shades redder as I let out a nervous laugh. The two women looked at one another and let out hardier laughs. "I'm just kidding, doll. You can bring the scale in the next room."

Through my sheepish smile, I mustered a thanks. I scooped up the scale, brought it into the next room, disrobed, and hopped on that scale. It flashed "164," confirming it was correctly calibrated, or at least calibrated to the three other scales I was using back home.

"What's the verdict?" one of the nurses asked from the next room.

"A hundred and sixty-four pounds."

"Oh, that's not bad. I would have guessed more given how muscular you are."

I nervously laughed again. "Thanks, still have to take off ten pounds by four p.m. tomorrow."

"Oh honey, that's too light, and too much weight to lose in such a short amount of time."

"Necessary evil of our sport I'm afraid. If I didn't bother to cut this weight, I'd be at a severe disadvantage, having to fight a much bigger opponent. I do appreciate the concern, but rest assured I've been doing this since I was thirteen years old and my doctor dad and nurse mom are sure to tell me how dumb the practice is. I'm right on track though."

"OK, well be safe."

"Will do. Will you guys be open in about two hours or so? I'd like to check my weight after my sauna session."

"We'll be here, cutie."

Still blushing I said, "Thanks, see you soon!"

And with that, I was off to shed some more weight.

The goal was to drop five to seven pounds, leaving just a few pounds to lose the day of the fight. I turned on the sauna, pulled up my weight loss playlist and sweat to the oldies—well relative oldies. Now, I'm not sure if this sauna was just hotter than the one I was accustomed to, or if I was just feeling extra dehydrated—probably a combination—but I usually was able to endure my 50-minute playlist with no issue. In that time, I generally would lose between five and seven pounds. However, I was struggling to endure more than 5-10 minutes at a time. I would sit in the sauna for about two songs, counting down the seconds, and then desperately exit to catch my breath and try to cool off some without fully losing my sweat. Also, I had been used to instantaneously sweating once I had entered a sauna. Given my hydration levels, it took about five minutes before I even began to sweat this time. All the more reason to walk that tightrope of cooling my body temperature without losing my sweat. I suffered through the whole session cutting in and out. But I did it. A quick rinse, a proper towel off for an accurate weight measurement, and I was back to the nurse's station.

"How it'd go, sweetie?"

"I'll let you know after the scale tells me," I tiredly responded.

Yikes. Only 160. All that for a measly four lbs.

"It went ok," I said half-resigned. "Six more pounds to go and I should float a pound or two in my sleep. I was hoping to have taken off a little more so I could eat and drink some, but alas I will have go without. What time do you guys open tomorrow, so I can time weighing myself?"

"Oh no hun, we're closed on the weekend."

I stared at the lady. "The casino doesn't offer health services on the weekend? Conceivably the busiest time for a casino?"

"Yeah, we don't get it either, but we don't make the rules."

"Hmm, is there any way I gain access to the room to

weight myself tomorrow?"

"We can't allow that for liability reasons; we have meds in here and such. But, since you're so cute, we can chance leaving the scale right outside the room if you promise not tell our boss." She winked.

"I promise, and thank you a ton! Well, I better get back to my room and try and get some rest. Thank you again for all of your help!"

"Good luck tomorrow!"

"Thanks ladies," I waved goodbye and headed off.

"Wait! What's your name so we can tell everyone that we met and helped you before you became famous?"

I flashed that coy smile again. "Dave Greenberg, or maybe Meanberg." This time I winked. "Thanks again!"

Nineteen

Stacking Odds in My Favor

I made it back to my room, feeling drawn out, sucked out, and weak, but happy to be on track. My plan now was to familiarize myself with the venue. After changing, I set off back through the casino out on to the Atlantic City boardwalk. It was after sunset, and there was a warm breeze coming off the ocean. I couldn't help but think to myself that the three-mile round trip would also help me shed a few ounces. On the 30-minute walk to get to Resorts Hotel and Casino, I made note that the walk would be harder tomorrow and even more drawn out and that I should be selective on the nutrients I brought with me as to not have a repeat transferring my gear from my car to my room. I took in the sights from the beach to all the diverse casinos and made it to Resorts. It was smaller than I imagined. I entered through the boardwalk entrance and began to look for signs for the Superstar Theater.

Sure, I wasn't the solo act, marquee, or even the headliner for the night of fights, but tomorrow I would comprise part of the cast, drawing people to the show. I dreamt I was the superstar, and it wasn't totally delusional, seeing how I would be drawing the most viewers—albeit for their love and support, not for any earned credential in this arena or any other fighting arena for that matter.

Following the meandering signs pointing me to the theater, it eventually led through a channeled-off corridor where spectators would ultimately be funneled. And there it was—an illuminated and backlit art deco, giant star with the words "The Superstar Theater" cutting through it, flanked by the New Breed Fighters Mixed Martial Arts Promotional poster for the event I was to perform and compete in. I took a moment to take it in. This shunted-off part of the casino had the eerie stillness to penetrate my soul. I envisioned the hordes of fight fans that would be dominating the now quiet scene less than 24 hours from then. Directly across the hall from the theater was the fighter staging area held in the Ocean Ballroom. *There is something oddly poetic about that,* I thought. I opened the unlocked door to view a mostly empty room with a few dividers set up. I exited to the front of the theater's grand entrance and reverently walked up to it like Arthur must have to Excalibur. I slowly wrapped my fingers around the handle and time slowed down. I collected my thoughts as I was about to reveal my destined arena of battle. I visualized this moment as a homecoming of sorts. I felt a jolt of electricity run through me, ready for the reveal. With the authority of a not yet crowned king, I powerfully pulled on the handle, as if the act itself would cement my legacy. *Click. Clank.* Time sped back up, as the latch assembly smashed against the strike-plate, denying entry. *Well that's embarrassing. It's locked.* Reverting and regressing to childlike curiosity, I pressed my face up against the doors to peer through the crack, merely to glimpse my destined altar of battle. There it was—and even though it

55

was barely viewed through a slit in the door into a poorly lit theater, my heart still skipped a beat.

Not yet satisfied, I went to track down a security guard with a key.

"Hi sir, would by any chance you be able to let me into the Superstar Theater?"

"If you left something behind you're best off going down to the lost and found to pick it up."

"Oh, no sir. I didn't lose anything. I am actually one of the fighters for the event tomorrow, and I was hoping to familiarize myself with the venue."

"If I don't let you in are you just going to kick my ass, take my keys and let yourself in anyhow? I best just help you out huh?" he chuckled to himself.

"In all seriousness, I have tons of respect for you guys who put it all on the line climbing into that cage. I mean you're crazy, but I respect it."

I let out a hearty laugh. "Thanks, yeah I can't really argue with that."

We walked back over to the theater entrance, and he pulled out his enlarged key ring, selected the correct one, and opened the door.

"Now I'm not supposed to leave you here alone, but you seem like a trustworthy guy. Just pull the door shut when you leave and make sure it latches. It will lock automatically."

"You got it. Thanks so much for all your help."

"Break a leg tomorrow...your opponent's." He chucked his distinctive chuckle and left me to soak in the environment.

There the cage was awaiting all of tomorrow night's action. For now, it was just me and her. I approached her like an altar—slow, deliberate, and with reverence. The cage door was open, and I took off my shoes and socks so I would be able to feel the canvas under my feet. I closed my eyes, visualizing the place packed and the deafening roar of the crowd, and centered my focus. I stepped in, noticing the canvas was more padded than I had anticipated. I then side-shuffled around the cage and pressed my back into the cage to feel it's resistance. I visualized again, this time my opponent making his entrance into the cage. I heard the referee shout, "Fight!" and engaged in shadow boxing. After about a minute of that, I raised my arms in victory, facing out to the imaginary audience. I took a moment to focus hard, imprinting that feeling deep into my subconscious. I exited the cage, put on my socks and shoes, and left the theater, making sure the door was locked behind me. Tired and drained from the weight cut on my half-hour walk back to the Tropicana, I was taking in the Atlantic City sights at night when a realization dawned on me—I was less than 24 hours away from testing the hypothesis that I wasn't ready when I signed up for this fight or when I broke the news to my trainer—but I would be. I felt ready, I thought, or maybe just delusional from dehydration.

Twenty

Modestly Modest

I tossed and turned all night. When my alarm went off at 8 a.m., I did not feel particularly well rested, but I still had some weight to take off. After hitting snooze a couple times, I roused my already dried-out bones to make my way to the scale and then the sauna yet again. I made it to the floor with the nurses' station, and as the elevator opened, I realized I was relying on the whim of the nurses' memory to leave the scale out, and the goodwill of any passersby to not steal the thing. I turned the corner, which revealed the entryway of the nurses' station. To my great relief, the corridor was as empty as last time, with the scale right outside the door as the nurse promised. I hop on, and "157" flashed...I was in the 150s for the first time since my freshman year of high school! *Sweet, now shut up and sweat,* I thought—three more to go.

You guys know the drill by now—I went to the sauna, put on my odd playlist, struggled to sweat since I was low on water, and managed to do it anyhow. Exiting the sauna felt like taking that first breath after you've been underwater for that split second too long. A sip of water would feel like pure ecstasy. That would have to wait for now. I elected to go back to my room to shower this time. While showering, I used cold water to cool my body temperature down. It took all of my willpower not to drink the water coming out of that shower head. I did, however, take mouthfuls and spit it out. Showered up and toweled off, I put a comfy pair of shorts and a T-shirt on and made my way back to that scale. It was about noon at this point, and if I were not on weight, it would be totally devastating.

Pushing the elevator call button to make my way back to the scale, I thought about how my friends and family would be arriving soon. I didn't dilly-dally, for I did not want to see them. I had to focus on my task at hand. "We don't bring our family or friends to war with us." Well, some say thoughts manifest reality, and as if that elevator button was actually a summon button to the universe for what I was hoping to avoid, the next stop revealed not less than 10 of my friends entering the elevator. My heart sank. Now of course I love my friends and am overly grateful for their support—but I was trying to get through this weight cut and muster up a killer mode in myself. Thankfully, the casino and in turn the elevator was far busier than it had been the day before. There must have been about five people on the elevator before my friends had walked in, and I was able to ever so slyly disappear into the background. It worked! All of my friends didn't recognize me. My stop was before the main casino floor so I was planning to make a swift, concise move to escape the elevator as soon as the door opened at my floor. *Blast!*

That same busyness now had the elevator stopping at almost every floor, prolonging my exposure. *C'mon! C'mon! C'mon!* I was thinking. *Stay cool.* My friends, for the most part, were lost in their own excitement and conversation. I was sort of just looking down, counting down for my stop to arrive. You ever get that feeling you're being watched or you're spotted? Well, my buddy Brad was off to the side, not participating in the conversation. I had that feeling in his general direction and using my peripheral vision, I couldn't rule out he hadn't made me. Slowly I brought my gaze up from the floor to his shit-eating grin. Then we locked eyes. I go to signal him the international sign of "please keep this quiet" by placing my index finger over my lips. Well Brad didn't even have to blow my cover as my motioning tipped off Chris. Chris did a double or triple take as he looked me over.

"Dave?! Is that really you?!" Brad burst out laughing, with his notorious tears forming as he laughed.

"Oh, hey guys," I said in an embarrassed and resigned voice.

Chris exclaimed, "Holy cow man, you don't look like anything like yourself."

None of my friends had seen me since Adam's birthday just over two months ago. In that relatively short amount of time, I was able to go from being out of shape to the absolute best shape of my life. I had noticed myself becoming more fit, but the visual change hadn't been as pronounced for me because I had seen myself every day as the transformation happened. My friends had seen me two months ago and the transformation that had happened in that time exceeded their expectations. Surely, they thought I'd be in shape. They had seen me in shape before, but not like this, and not in this short amount of time. It just goes to show, when you really commit yourself to something and go full force, you can move mountains (of fat at least) more quickly than you might think. In Chris' disbelief of the speed of my makeover, he reflexively lifted my shirt to expose my trim stomach. I was proud of it, but it was a tad uncomfortable having a man lift my shirt in public to gawk, even if it was a close heterosexual friend.

"Whoa whoa whoa, Chris what are you doing? Please let go of my shirt."

All of our friends burst out laughing. "Chris what are you doing?" a few of our friends said in concert.

Chris realized what he was doing and let out a nervous laugh. "Whoops sorry. You just don't look anything like, well, you."

"Thanks, I think," I laughed.

"Wait, have you been in here the whole time?"

"Well seeing how the elevator only has the one door, yep. I've been back here."

"Right, well why didn't you say anything when we walked in then?"

"Yeah, so I was sort of hoping to avoid everyone until after the fight. I'm trying to focus on getting in the zone. The only reason I'm even out of my room is because I have to check to make sure I am on weight. But, since my cover is blown, why don't you guys come with me?"

My friends were all excited to be a part of the prefight preparation and enthusiastically followed me to the nurses' station for what hopefully would be my last weight check before the official weigh-in.

As we neared the scale outside of the nurses' station, there was a noticeable difference this time apart from all other times I went to go weigh myself. Namely, there were crowds of people in the hallway now. My friends stood around, looking perplexed as to why I wasn't hopping on the scale.

Brad piped up. "What are you waiting for, dude? Go ahead, weigh yourself."

"You see, the thing is, I've been weighing myself naked this whole time. And while I'm sure the many casino security cameras had a view, it wasn't in front of a live audience."

With friends as true as mine, it was no surprise they all laughed and said, "So? Get on with it, sissy." I stepped on the scale with all of my clothes on, and the screen flashed 155.5. Now I was reasonably confident I was under 154 without my clothes on, and even more sure I was under 155 (we do get a 1 lb. weight allowance), but I did want to make the actual weight class, and I wanted to be sure I was under the limit, not merely reasonably sure.

"What's it say?" one of my friends queried.

"A hundred fifty-five point five. I'm probably fine. I'd feel much better if I knew for sure though. Would you guys mind forming a wall around me as I strip down and check?"

Without a spoken word, the group of them lined up in formation, shoulder to shoulder, reveling in their usefulness and calling more attention than needed by shouting, "Nothing to see here folks! Keep it moving! Want to take a picture? It'd last longer, ma'am!"

"Chris no peaking!" I teased, following up his shirt-lifting incident.

Appreciating swiftness to be an asset, I disrobed like a virginal adolescent who gets the go ahead from his girlfriend for the first time. I leapt onto the scale, and 153 appeared on the display. I put on my clothes like that teenager might have if his girlfriend's father walked in.

"Done! Thanks!"

"How's your weight?"

"One pound under. Good to go. I don't mean to be rude gentleman, but I am going to excuse myself so that I can begin to get into the zone as I prepare for battle." I could sense my friends wanted me to stick around. I was appreciative that they didn't give me a tough time for departing though.

I went back to my room to avoid running into anyone else I knew. I took this time to relax and connect with my trainer, who would be driving down from North Jersey (two hours away) to corner me. It was about two p.m., two hours away from weigh-ins, when I got in touch with Brian.

"Hey Brian, just wanted to get your ETA for when you'd be down here by?"

"When is the fighter meeting again?"

"Fighter meeting is at six, but the weigh-ins are at four."

"OK. I should be able to take off here around four."

"Oh, you won't be here for the weigh-ins?"

"Nah, you don't need me there for that. How's your weight? How much did you cut?"

"I cut sixteen pounds over two days. I just weighed myself, and I'm on weight—under a little, so long as their scale is properly calibrated."

"Great job man! See you at the fighter meeting."

"Thanks, uh, ok see you then."

"Wait, which casino is it again?"

"Resorts."

"Which way is that on the strip when exiting the Atlantic City Expressway again?"

"It's to the left, north on the boardwalk."

"Right. Thanks. See you soon. Good work on the weight cut."

It was a little unsettling that Brian wouldn't be there for the weigh-in. What if there was some fishy business? It was also unsettling that he'd be leaving with exactly enough time to make the fighter meeting and that he didn't remember where the fight was or how to get there. Good thing I wasn't risking my physical health in my first ever cage fight, otherwise I might have begun to unravel. There was no sense in worrying over things out of my control. Instead, I put my focus on packing for my weigh-in. I planned to leave an hour later to get there early and weigh myself on their scale to check for any discrepancies. I packed a small bag with a water bottle, sports drink, energy bars, fruit, and a pair of sweats in case I was off weight on their scale—we were allowed an hour to make weight if we didn't make it after the initial weigh-in. With the bag packed and an hour until weigh-ins, it was time to take off.

I took the same walk as the one I took the night before, careful to travel alertly to avoid any contact with any supporters descending on the city. There was one glaring difference from my walk last night though—just like how I had noticed the casino had become more crowded, so too had the Atlantic City boardwalk. As I closed in on Resorts Casino, I was accosted with loud music and a DJ. There was a huge tent set up and gigantic speakers pumping out music. It was summer after all, and I figured the casino was running a boardwalk beach party. As I got closer, I saw all the fight promotion's logos and gear all over the place. This was to attract attention to the event tonight. *That's cool,* I thought to myself as I went to move pass and make my way inside to find where the weigh-ins would be, oblivious to the fact that that was to be the location for the weigh-ins. I was eventually clued in as I was headed beyond it all and had to step over a couple of scales. *Oh right, this is where the weigh-ins are to be held.* An MC got on the mic and began promoting the fights, announcing tickets could be purchased inside. Us fighters were going to have to strip down on the crowded Atlantic City boardwalk— we were to be the props, and I guess sexy bodies sell. *Gulp.*

Thirty minutes until I had to drop my knickers in front of hundreds of people. Well, it was best I made sure I was on weight—no need to add to my mortification by finding out I missed weight for the first time in front of everyone. I took off my sneakers and stepped on the scale as it read 152. I was two whole pounds under?! Three with the allowance?! I took out my sports drink, stepped on the scale again, this time holding it to make sure I didn't drink too much and then put myself over. Now I cannot confirm this, but it's hard for me to believe that all of the five scales I had been using were all off by the same margin, and that this state-regulated scale was the only correct one. It seemed to me that they wanted to prevent fighters from missing weight. I was a little pissed off about that because I actually made the weight limit and now I was worried my opponent would come in at 155 on *their* scale and really be 157. Again, just another thing that was out of my control.

The waiting around was anxiety producing. Furthering my unease was that as fighters were showing up, they were showing up with not only their trainers, but their entire teams too. I was there all alone. I didn't have my trainer or a training partner, much less my entire team with me. I was seriously starting to regret not having my friends I bumped into in the elevator come with me as my entourage. Even if it was the same crew that didn't get involved in the five-on-one beat down I suffered, their presence and moral support would have been tons more than I had standing there all by myself, leaning on a wall. Just then I felt someone put their hand on my shoulder and say, "Yo Juice, you think you're some sort of tough guy?"

Startled and already on edge, I quickly turned to see who was affronting me. A wave a relief washed over me as I saw my smirking Uncle Tony. I don't know how he spotted me in the sea of fighters, but I was sure glad he did. I pointed out to him who my opponent was—I recognized him from the fight video and social media creeping I had done. He was dressed rather unassumingly, quite frankly presented as a cross between a punk (fashion-wise, not behavior wise) and a gentleman. He was with about five other guys, more or less giving off the same vibe.

My uncle joked, "So he's the guy you're going to beat his fists up with your face huh?"

Ha-ha Uncle Tony. Ha-Ha.

I was so grateful for Uncle Tony easing my nerves and passing the time. The MC got back on the mic, and I looked up to see the place truly packed. There were many fighters, even more fighter support teams, and fans and passersby on the boardwalk, angling for a better view. The proceedings were underway. Fighters were being called up, stripping to their underwear, stepping on the scale, and giving their best pose before being recycled in for the next fighter to go through the same procedure. Initially I was unsure if they were going to square opponents up with one another for a stare down—an opportunity to properly size up who we were going to fight. Gearing up for that proved to be an exercise in futility as there were to be no stare downs. Still, the ability to observe my opponent's movements and survey his physique did provide an opportunity to acquire data—sizing up complete, I was feeling confident. It was my turn to face the scale. I walked up, disrobed, hopped on the scale at 153.8 lbs., flexed my abs a bit (you know, nothing too showy or obvious), had my picture taken, and put my clothes back on. Quite unceremonious considering the hundreds in attendance and it being my first time in my underwear in a public forum. Just like that, it was all over.

Twenty-one

Não Me Julgue por Este Aluno

I walked back to the Tropicana with a new pep in my step, nourished by the natural mana of the world, water and fruit—and sports drinks and power bars. I don't know what it was, but that southward walk on the Atlantic City boardwalk made my awareness that it was time to fight more evident. Maybe it was just passing various milestones. Not only was my awareness heightened to the looming fight, but time seemed to accelerate over this passage as well.

By the time I made it back to my room, I had scant time to continue to refuel my body, pack and grab all of my gear, and head back over to Resorts Casino. I was loaded more like that pack mule I had been when I first arrived to AC the day before, but at least I was feeling stronger from the food and drink. I thought to myself, though, that next fight I ought to stay at the casino I was fighting in. Chris did get a good group rate for all of us, and I was relieved that I didn't have to handle that end of the organizing. Still, I made the note to do it differently next time. Humping gear across that boardwalk one more time in the summer heat had me sweating to the point where I may have been able to make weight all over again.

I made it into the casino and went down the shunted-off hallway to the where the Superstar Theater, the fighter check-in, and the staging area all were. I dumped my gear in the staging area and went to check in. When I got to check-in, they asked where my trainer was. I informed them that he was currently underway and should be here shortly. It was about 5:30 at this point, and they were quick to point out that there were only 30 minutes left to meet the deadline to check in. I felt another bead of sweat drip down my forehead—as if I wasn't sweating enough already. I excused myself to go call Brian.

"Hey man, we're cutting it close to the wire here. The fight promotion reps are telling me I won't be able to fight unless we check in together in the next thirty minutes."

"Relax man, I'm fifteen minutes away. Besides, they're just saying that; they'll let you fight."

I can't say I found much of that reassuring. "OK man, I'm right across from the Superstar Theater. I'll wait here for you."

Fifteen minutes went by, and I got a call from Brian. "Hey man, I'm pulling into the parking garage. Do you know how to get to the theater from here, or which entrance I should use?"

"No, I came in from the boardwalk entrance."

"Shit, I should have asked the parking garage attendant."

Deciding to take the bull by the horns, I told Brian, "I'll

come find you and walk you here. That's probably easiest. What section are you in?"

"Sweet, thanks. I'll park in section F on the second level."

"F2 got it! I'll be right there!" Ticked off without the time for it, I literally went running after my trainer.

I found his worn and aging pickup truck in the parking lot. Brian got out and said, "Damn traffic. Anyway, congrats again on cutting the weight."

"Thanks man. OK follow me," I said in a hurry.

"Dude, you worry too much. I've been down this road countless times. They're just using scare tactics. They will not stop you from fighting."

"OK got it. It's right this way."

Before we could even exit the parking garage, Brian spotted who he thought was a famous Brazilian fighter headed the same way as us.

"Yo, I think that's [whoever he said]."

"Cool, who's that?" I asked, as I continued to walk hurriedly, as if I had an invisible lasso around Brian that might expedite us getting to check-in.

"You serious? He's a famous Jiu-Jitsu fighter."

"Oh cool, so I think it's up that escalator over there and then a short walk and we're there."

"I've been practicing my Portuguese for a moment just like this."

Seriously?!

"A moment when we're running late to a check-in?"

"You worry too much."

Brian slowed his walk so that this guy I'd never heard of could catch up.

"Oi [whoever it was], como vai? Eu sou um grande fã."

"Obrigado. Você conhece portugues?"

"Só um pouco. Eu sou um instructor de Jiu-Jitsu e MMA."

"Estou aqui para treinar um dos meus alunos na luta desta noite."

"Esse é o seu aluno?" The Brazilian fighter pointed to me.

Brian squirmed a little bit and said, "Sim, mas essa é apenas a primeira luta dele. Eu treino muitos lutadores profissionais, um mesmo no UFC."

Now I don't speak Portuguese, so the above is my estimation of how things went, but I'd bet a hefty amount I am not far off. You shouldn't need to speak Portuguese either to get the vibe. The Brazilian fighter didn't answer Brian. He looked at me, extended his hand to shake mine, and said in a thick Portuguese accent, "Good luck tonight. Fight hard." It was as if he said, "You have a harder road ahead if your own trainer is ashamed of you." I was already ticked off, but what this did was cement for me the fact that it was just going to be me in that cage fighting my opponent. I was confident and needed nothing more than myself to rely on.

We finally made it to the fighter registration. As they were taking my paperwork, the employee commented, "Wow, you guys just made it. If it were another five more minutes you would have been closed out." I shot a look over to Brian.

"Wow you guys are a lot stricter than some of your competitors," Brian exclaimed, surprised.

Paperwork submitted, walkout music turned over, and that took care of that—or so I thought. I had forgotten about the doctor's clearance. I was already unnerved from barely making the deadline getting here. That served as a bit of distraction from the anxiety I had been feeling from that looming clearance. What came flooding back into my memory as the employee directed me to the doctor station was that cut I had suffered less than two weeks ago that I had glued shut myself, hiding in my eyebrow. Additionally, I was worried that he may notice that I couldn't make my left arm go completely straight (I still can't) from when my elbow had been popped way back in the beginning of my training camp. All he did was take my pulse as he asked,

"Any injuries or concerns?"

"Nope!" I lied enthusiastically.

"OK, you're good to go."

Wow that was easy, I thought to myself, perhaps a little too easy for the likes of a cage fight. Aww well, no point tempting fate, right? As I got up to go confer with Brian (It was nice to finally have him there to take some of the pressure off me), the registrar scolded me.

"Make sure you are not late for the rules meeting. It starts at seven o'clock sharp. If you miss it, you will not be able to fight—no ifs, ands, or buts."

"OK, thanks for your help."

"All checked in," I said relieved to Brian.

"Sweet, I'm starving. Let's go find something to eat."

A quick word on Brian's appearance: He was about 5'10", had shaved his head bald, and sported a ginger circle-beard and a beer belly. That day he was wearing black athletic shorts, white sneakers, a navy blue backward Yankees hat, and a black t-shirt accented with red lettering, displaying his martial arts school logo. That beer belly driving Brian to get food now took my focus, instead of where it belonged, on getting in the zone.

"Are you sure we have enough time?" I asked rhetorically.

Spoken with unfounded confidence he reflexively responded, "Yeah, we'll be back with plenty of time. So, what's good to eat around here?"

"Uh I don't know. I haven't been eating anything other than the food I brought, and I haven't been staying at this casino."

"OK we'll find something."

Thankfully, there was a restaurant not too far from the theater.

"How's here?" I ask somewhat desperately.

"Well let me look at the menu."

Jesus Christ! I thought to myself.

After taking five minutes to peruse the menu, Brian

found it agreeable. After sitting down, the waitress handed us menus and took our drink order. "OK, I'll be right back." Five minutes elapsed, then 10, and after we were 15 minutes in, we only had 15 minutes to be at the fighter meeting.

"Uh Brian, do you think we're going to have enough time to make it back to the rules meeting?"

"When is it?"

"7:00 *sharp*." I emphasized the sharp for good reason.

He looked at his watch. "Shit, man that's in fifteen minutes. No we don't have time to wait here."

"I did notice they had hot dogs on the boardwalk."

"I'm not really in the mood for hot dogs, but I guess they'll have to do."

Seriously?! Like what the hell?

We made our way down to the boardwalk, and I was watching the time like a hawk.

"OK the hot dog stand is right there."

"Wait, what's that down there?" Fifty yards away there was another stand, but it had a line of people. "Let's go check that one out."

"Are sure we have enough time?"

"Definitely. You worry too much."

Grrrr!

"Kielbasa sausage, oh yeah that's much better."

We got in line and there were only two people ahead of us. One guy in front took forever to apply the fixings to each sausage. It was taking *forever*. Finally, Brian got to the counter. "Can I get two of the sausages?"

TWO?!

The cage fight later was looking like it wouldn't be my first fight of the day. How was it possible he could be so inconsiderate as to be a cause of stress in what was the most stressful endeavor I had ever signed up for? It was five minutes to 7:00 now.

"Can you eat those as we walk to the rules meeting?"

"I don't like to walk while I eat. It gives me

indigestion."

#!$!#@!!!!!

I watched him sloppily scarf down the sausage, managing to get mustard and whatever else all down his shirt with his own school's logo—great advertising. He took his last bite, wiped his mustarded face with the tiny napkin the vendor had provided, not quite getting it all, and we headed back in. We arrived five minutes late, and thankfully the door wasn't locked. The stares we got for being late to this rules meeting were more than piercing. If Brian making us late wasn't bad enough, I had to walk in with this mustard-covered fool. Thankfully it was just a formality for me that we barely slid by on—I had studied the rules on my own. At the conclusion of the meeting, Brian excused himself to the restroom to wash the remaining mustard off his soul.

Twenty-two

Afghan Hound in Elephant Tusk Clothing

After the fighters' meeting, Brian and I returned to our staging area. As soon as we arrived, Brian received a phone call.

"OK sweet. Yeah, we're right across from the Superstar Theater."

"Who was that?" I asked.

"Max, he's going to help me corner you."

Max was one of my training partners. He had damn good technique, and we would give each other some pretty serious battles in the gym. Max was also a bit of an oddball, but lovable nonetheless.

"OK we better start to tape up your hands. I don't

want you to have to worry about getting it done after the fighter introductions." Brian pulled up a chair next to mine and instructed me to flip my chair around—you know, like the edgy backward chair-sitting AC Slater does from *Saved by the Bell.*

I obliged and stuck out one of my hands to have it taped. It occurred to me that I had never had my hands taped before.

"Spread your fingers wide and stretch them upwards. Let me know if it's too tight."

Brian wrapped the first hand and then we repeated the process. Brian taped my hands in such a way so that they were not overly bulky. You may have noticed boxers' wraps are like clubs. Well that makes sense right—they swing for maximum impact.

By the way, a common misconception is that we wear gloves to protect our opponent by lessening the force of the impact from strikes. Truth is, we can hit with *more* force when we're wearing gloves, for the simple reason of the wraps underneath. The wraps and gloves are intended to protect the striker's hands and wrists. Without those wraps and gloves, a full-force blow to most parts of an opponent's head would cause injury to the hand or wrist—often breaking bones. Heck, that even sometimes happens with the wraps and gloves. The reason I elected to not have my wraps so built up was so that I would be able to grapple more efficiently—that after all was my strength. With less padding on my hands, I would be able to manipulate my grips more easily, and with a lower likelihood of my gloves getting snagged when going in for a move.

My buddy and training partner Max arrived just as my wraps were all complete. I must say that even though I elected for the smaller wraps, it did feel like I was donning two weapons—wrecking balls even. I liked how they felt. After greeting Max, we were called by the organizers to have our wraps inspected and then to head across the hall through the back entrance of the theater for fighter introductions. The commission representative took one look at my hands and asked,

"How come there's no gauze?"

"Uh I don't know."

"I can't approve this. You don't need a lot but, you do need to cover your knuckles with gauze."

"Umm ok, so should I skip the fighter introductions then?"

"Go to the fighter introductions, and then immediately after, have your hands rewrapped and find me again so I can approve them."

So much for that peace of mind.

As I was about to make my way over to the staging area for our fighter intros, Brian came running up. I figured he may have overheard the issue about the wraps, and he was going to offer some solace or reassurance that it was no big deal. Nope. He had a gym bag in tow, and he started rummaging through it. He pulled out a bright red t-shirt with his martial arts school logo on it.

"Dude put this on for the fighter introductions—free advertising."

I took off my shirt and put his on. "Brian! I'm swimming in this thing."

It was a 2x or 3xl easy and at 5'8" 165 lbs. (Now that I put back on some of the weight I cut), that thing was legit down to my knees.

"You look, great kid. Go get 'em!"

"Wait, my wraps weren't approved. The commission said there needs to be some amount of gauze in the wrap."

"What? Really? I've never heard of that. Don't worry, we'll get it straightened out after the fighter intros."

And with that, I ran off to catch up with the rest of the fighters. I found my way to the staging area where all the fighters were lined up. As I was asking one of the fighters towards the back if introductions were by weight order or fight order, I heard my name being called out repeatedly and in quick succession from a woman holding a clipboard. "Dave Greenberg? *Dave Greenberg? Dave Greenberg?!*"

I called out, "Here!" as if I was back in grade school being marked down for attendance.

"Geeze man, where were you?"

"Uh well I…"

She cut me off.

"It's not important. Just stand here next to your opponent and when your name is called, walk out, pause, pose for the live-feed camera, and then walk through the crowd back to the staging area across the hall. Got it?"

Before I could answer, she was already walking away. It was a bit awkward having to be in such close proximity to my opponent. There was a weird energy—a sort of hybrid of posturing while maintaining a sort of cool attitude. The ring girls flanking us only served to heighten the awkward multifaceted dynamic. Let's just say an already testosterone-rich environment was further fueled by very attractive women wearing next to nothing. We were held in that pen for longer than any of us would have liked—especially once the women were called to the stage before the rest of us. The announcer called our names one by one like the strangest commencement ceremony you would have ever seen. My name was called, and I walked out on to the stage and gave my best fighter's pose for the camera, and my army of supporters went wild. My opponent was called after me, and said army unleashed their boos. I moved to walk off the stage when someone grabbed me by the arm. Was my opponent pissed off at all the boos and wanting to get our night started early? Nope, it was a man in his 50s or 60s in an over-the-top ivory suit, gaudy gold jewelry, sunglasses, and the most striking pin-straight, shiny white hair that flowed all the way down to his lower back.

"Hey kid. It's me Scott. Good luck tonight."

I gave him a point to acknowledge him and made my

way through the crowd as they cheered me on even harder.

Twenty-three

Turning On

I made it back across the hall to the fighter staging area, anxious to get my wraps (re)taken care of. Brian for the first time was showing he was a bit frazzled, as he hurriedly had me sit down to cut off the wraps and begin again. Wraps cut off, he pulled out the tape and attempted to pull a wingspan-long piece from the roll when it broke free halfway.

"Shit, this roll is done." Brian started rummaging through his bag to pull out another roll. "Shit! This can't be! How can this be?!"

"What man? What's going on?"

"I can't seem to find any more tape."

"You only brought half of a roll of tape?! Are you serious?!"

"Don't worry. I'll send Max out to the local pharmacy to get more."

"We don't have time for that!"

Taking matters into my own hands, I walked over to one of the fighters and his trainer as he was getting his hands taped.

"Hey man, this is really embarrassing, but you wouldn't happen to have any extra tape I can buy off you?"

"This is why I pack multiple rolls—always be prepared." His trainer tossed me a full roll.

"Dude, thank you so much! What do I owe you?"

"Don't worry about it. Just focus on your fight. Can't have my tape losing any fights tonight." He winked as I scurried back to Brian for him to start taping my hands again.

75

"See man, I told you—you had nothing to worry about. It'd all work out."

It takes just about all the discipline I can muster not to roll my eyes—good thing martial arts helps with that.

With my hands re-taped, I made my way back over to the commission. With one quick look to see that there was now gauze over my knuckles, he signed my wraps, signifying they were approved. Upon receiving the news that my wraps had been approved, Brian flippantly said, "Told you, kid. There was nothing to stress about." My eye-rolling discipline was really being tested at that point. But it held up—perhaps I could offer some seminars on the technique.

Brian then pulled out a jump rope from his bag and handed it to me.

"OK kid. It's time to warm up." There were closed-circuit TVs scattered around the room broadcasting the fights across the hall. Knowing where we were on the fight card, we were able to use the information of who was fighting to gauge when to begin getting ready.

"Brian, why are you giving me a jump rope to warm up?"

"You gotta start to break a sweat kid."

I understood that, but none of my training leading up to the fight did he or I incorporate jumping rope. I was feeling that I wanted to keep to things that were familiar, find some comfort in ritual and normalcy. I mean, the fight hadn't even happened. I had to deal with numerous curveballs already. I guessed the more curveballs you saw, the better you got at hitting them. I began to jump rope, despite not having done it in years. After the first few attempts, I realized that the jump rope itself was way too long for my 5'8" frame. I began to tie knots in it to shorten the length. That worked and all, but with being out of practice, I struggled to find a rhythm, my cadence was all off, and I felt foolish and frustrated. I threw the damn rope back into the bag in front of Brian.

"Forget that thing. I haven't been jumping rope this whole time leading up to this fight. I'm not going to start now."

"You gotta break a sweat kid."

"I'll do it my way."

And with that, I made yet another executive decision and began shadow boxing. It was odd to be warming up in such an open space in front of all of the other fighters. I was still feeling like a bit of an imposter never having done this before. I tried to put that out of my mind and kept with my routine. What made it most difficult to focus, though, was across the way I saw my opponent toggle between warming up himself and pacing while he stared me down. I returned the favor, even if only it was a mask. A new feeling was welling up inside—a healthy concoction of fear, anxiety, thrill, and purpose. I had a mission where I would be risking life and limb. One's body responds to this. I did my best to manage my physiology—aware that an "adrenaline dump" too soon could cost me the fight. And for the nerves? Rob Gilbert put it best. "It's all right to have butterflies in your stomach. Just get them to fly in formation."

With the conclusion of one fight on the card, it meant that the fight before mine was starting, and I was on deck. I was approached by the commission to go to the final warm-up staging area. On the way over, we were directed through a bunch of fold-out tables with loads of equipment laid out on them. It felt like gladiators being presented with their choice of weapon before battle.

"Pick out the shin guards and gloves you like."

"Oh, thanks, but I have my own I'll be using."

"What are you talking about? You can't use yours."

"Uh, I was told by the fight promotion's owner that I was eligible to use my own so long as they met the specifications."

"Yeah you could have, but you would have needed to do that at the beginning of the fighters' meeting. Why didn't you do it then?"

I shot Brian a perturbed expression. "Oh, I guess it must have been the nerves that stole my attention." I didn't break eye contact with Brian as I was talking to the commission.

"Alright man. Hurry up and get your equipment. We can squeeze in the approval."

"Thanks!" I exclaimed as I ran back to the staging area to grab my gear. After a hurried look over, my equipment was approved. I was instructed to gear up. My gloves and shin guards were tapped to hold them in place, and my gloves were signed over the tape to indicate there was no tampering. Brian, Max, and I were then directed to the final warm-up area. The warm-up section was cordoned off from the rest of the fighters. There were mats laid out allowing for a proper warm-up. It wasn't until now that I allowed myself to flip the switch. What switch you ask? *The* switch.

Twenty-four

Meditation on Flipping the Switch

Only once in my life was I forced to snap a limb of an opponent. It was in a small dojo tournament, *The Long Island Ironman Brazilian Jiu-Jitsu Open*. I hadn't been training for about half a year, but I was in pretty good shape working in a gym as a personal trainer. I remember getting to the tournament and catching up with some old friends I hadn't seen in a while. After we exchanged pleasantries, it was time to warm-up. At this time, I took it upon myself to mentally prepare for my goal of winning the thing. I told myself, *I am not here for anything less than first, not even second will do.* Simultaneously I was readying my body and must have had my game face on as I was preparing to undertake my first tournament win of any kind. One of my friends saw the seriousness of the look in my eyes as I was warming up.

He leaned over to me and said, "Dude, you gotta calm down."

In one of the most profound moments of clarity in my life to that point, I turned, looked him dead in the eye, and said, "No, that is not what I need right now."

I must have spooked him because he quickly retreated. And, it turns out, that was the truth as I would go on to win my first tournament ever of any kind. But, before I could win the tournament—I had to win my mindset. I had tapped into something I never had tapped into before. I found my switch.

In the first match of the tournament, I achieved a dominant position over my opponent and began working towards a submission. I secured what's called an Americana, or key lock submission (which is an attack on the shoulder joint), and slowly began to apply steady increasing pressure. My opponent was tough—especially mentally (surely a product of training martial arts no doubt) and was doing a good job of resisting my submission. Giving him every opportunity as I slowly ratcheted up the pressure, assuring his tap out, out of nowhere—he broke free. This is where I learned to turn on that new-found switch. Now what I'm about to share may sound a little cruel, but you have to understand that this was a high stakes contest. Given the opportunity, my opponent would show no hesitancy or mercy in finishing a submission. Furthermore, it takes a tremendous amount of energy to win a match. Now multiply that out over multiple matches to win a tournament. This guy could have had the decency to acknowledge defeat and tap out and send me on my way to winning the tournament, but, no, he just had to break free from my submission. So, this time when I slapped the submission back on, I didn't give him the option to tap out—I just went full beans from the onset. He resisted the best he could until his shoulder was torn out of his socket with a loud snap. I'm not proud of it, but he knew just as well as I did the risk of competing in a tournament like that. I can honestly say it was one of the most disturbing experiences I have had—and I don't mean solely from a moral paradigm either. The actual act of dislocating a man's shoulder was disgusting. It felt similar to pulling apart chicken bones, only bigger and way grosser. After the tournament was over, I saw my opponent in the locker room.

"Why didn't you tap out?

"I wanted to win," he answered simply.

And you know what? I could understand it and respected it.

I had let my friends and family know I was competing in the tournament, but discouraged them from coming, given its relatively small size. Also, my lack of preparation left me not as confident until I found my switch. My buddy Nick (not Pickles) was a former U.S. Army Ranger, and as tough as they come. He decided to show up to the tournament without telling me, and despite the relatively small number of spectators, you wouldn't have guessed how few people were there given how loud Nick was cheering for me alone.

There were actually two tournaments that day, Gi and No Gi (a Gi is the traditional martial arts garb). It was common for Brazilian Jiu-Jitsu tournaments to have both divisions, and many competitors competed in both. After winning that first tournament, I thought I would walk through the No Gi division no problem. What I didn't account for was losing that laser focus I had for the first tournament. That simple lapse in my focus allowed my "switch" to return to the default off position. In the semifinals of the second tournament, I got caught in a rare and fancy submission—a flying armbar. It should never have happened, and it wouldn't have if I kept my focus. It isn't every day that you're blessed with a lesson of that magnitude *and* earn a trophy the same day.

Happy to go home and shower up after a day of competing, my buddy Nick was having none of it. He rounded up a group of us friends, and we all went for dinner and drinks. Nick wasn't a particularly rich man, but he wouldn't let me pay for anything that night. His only condition was that I brought my trophy in with us wherever we went. I wasn't keen on letting him pay for me or bringing in my trophy for display. It was hard to argue with Nick—you try telling an Army Ranger otherwise. Besides, it wouldn't have mattered, everywhere we went he would introduce me to strangers as "The Champ" as he held up my trophy.

Twenty-five

It's Time

Throughout all of the beatings I took in training, specifically sparring with professional fighters—I told myself the difference when fight night rolled around would be my ability to flip that switch. Heck even to this day I don't love sparring, and to be honest don't fully understand it even. I mean sparring is to simulate fighting, but it is not fighting. Sparing also isn't charades. In karate, we would point spar, fully pulling our punches. In MMA sparring, our punches are pulled, but not fully. It is a fine line.

I dipped passed that line for the first time with Max as I was warming up only moments away from stepping into the cage. I wasn't hitting him, but in my mind's eye, I saw my fists breaking his glass jaw. I was here. I wanted this, right? There was ferocity in me that I started to let out. I summoned all the pain in my life and harnessed it to feed extra torque and power to my blows. It was an odd feeling to slowly unchain my inner beast. The beast was ferocious and anxious, ready to snap at anything perceived in its way. It was a weird limbo, the unchaining process. For I wouldn't be fully unleashed until that referee said, "Fight." Meanwhile, I noticed others becoming aware of my transformation. Brian began to see what had been in me all along. In training, I was very measured, astute, and cerebral. I was now calling on unbridled aggression to pull up a seat at that table. Brian worried I would experience that adrenalin dump and actually pulled me off my warm up.

"You cool man?"

"Yeah, just transforming into the version of myself that is about to get into a cage fight."

Prizefighting is a funny thing. Unlike when I was protecting my buddy Adam from those savages, I had nothing against my opponent—other than we were after the same dream: winning a prizefight in Atlantic City. Nonetheless, he posed a very real threat to my physical well-being and that was reason enough as far as I was concerned to open the door to the caged beast. When my trainer took his foot off the gas with my warm up, I started pacing, gnawing on my mouthpiece—literally chomping at the bit. I was mindful of controlling that adrenaline, at least the best that I could for my first ever cage fight. Unceremoniously a fight official approached us.

"It's time."

Twenty-six

The Stage is Set

Remember now, I was this mostly nerdy guy who signed up for a cage fight. As luck should have it the bout right before mine was an even nerdier guy than me with a body to show for it. Skillful in BJJ as I understood, which might be the most cerebral martial art there is.

The question was if his intellect and careful study of the "gentle art" were enough to surmount his opponent. Well, he was paired up with a hulk of a man. A real Goliath, which was fitting because the nerdy martial artist shared my namesake—David.

The audience (my supporters included) feared that this was a horrible mismatch. They all spouted,

"How can they be in the same weight class?"

The crowd was witnessing the real consequence when one fighter adhered to the controversial practice of weight cutting and the other did not. It was a true contest of brains versus brawn. I wasn't there to witness it, but as it was purported to me by my supporters, they watched something just a notch below a snuff film.

"His nose exploded, and was bleeding so much we were worried he'd pass out or bleed out."

Brawn had won out over brains in that contest. There was no mistaking this omen by those there for me. After they squeegeed as much of the blood off the canvas as they could, it would be my turn. A good number of my supporters ordered a few shots to drown out those surging nerves.

Twenty-seven

Dead Man Walking

Back to the commission official coming over to interrupt my warm up.

"It's time." *Oh man here we go.* A lifetime of work, setbacks, and resurgences had led me to this very point. *I wanted this, right?* Careful what you wish for. Brian, Max, and I were led through a back exit across a public hallway into a staging area where we waited to be announced. This was a grosser proposition than one might think. Being ushered through areas that were open to the public and having to take a circuitous route as to avoid said public lengthened the trip. So? You may ask. I did all this barefoot. It was a little weird, but I put it out of mind quickly as I was about to be locked in a cage with a man who had trained to inflict as much harm on me as possible. Pictures later showed that the bottoms of all the fighters' feet had been as black as a chimney sweep.

Calling where we were a staging area was a bit generous—we were in a back stairwell, listening into the theater for my announcement. Peering through a crack in the doorway, I glimpsed the full house for the first time. *Had I really done enough to earn this? Am I really ready?* I tried to put those thoughts out of my mind.

Meanwhile back in the arena, spectators were filing in. In the crowd so too were my supporters. One hundred strong in a sea of close to a couple of thousand. Most were donning their supportive Meanberg T-shirts. The "Mean" was green and had angry eyebrows over the vowels set against the black shirt.

Breaking through the din of the crowd, the announcer came on the loudspeaker. I started to bounce in rhythm, keeping the blood flowing and pumping myself up.

"Ladies and gentleman…"

OK here we go, I think to myself.

"Make sure you take a look at our menus to grab something to eat. We serve more than just drinks—tell your waitress."

"Jeez what a tease," Brian let out.

"You think?!" I snapped back.

A couple of more minutes went by as we stood in this dimly lit stairwell with my bare feet on the cold concrete. My cold feet were almost enough to give me cold feet. That, and I was worried about losing my sweat. Conventional wisdom states you should have broken a sweat before stepping into the cage. Well, I did, but nowhere in my training to date did they train me for this ice session right before the biggest moment of my life. The announcer came back on.

"OK finally," I sighed, and begin to bounce again.

"Has anyone found a wallet? We have a patron that lost their wallet. If you find it and turn it in, there is a fifty dollar reward you can collect."

"MOTHERFUCKER!" I screamed to the sky like a protagonist in an overly dramatized Hollywood movie scene, where the camera cuts and zooms out, repeating the echo first heard in the theater, to scaring off birds on the Atlantic City boardwalk, and finally to a shot of the Earth from space where the scream could still be heard.

"Whoa easy there, kid. Save some of that for the cage," Brian joked.

"So, what do we do if we find the wallet while I'm on my walkout? Do we abandon the walkout to turn in the wallet and collect our reward?" I snarkily retorted.

"OK man don't get too worked up. They'll be announcing you any second now," Brian mustered in his best comforting, obviously rarely used, tone.

And as if exactly scripted from that overly dramatized Hollywood movie, the announcer came back over the loudspeaker.

Part II

Opportunity

Twenty-eight

Can You Feel That?

"Two warriors bring in the super welterweight division. Fighting out of the blue corner, he stands in at five feet eight inches. Weighed in tonight at one hundred fifty-three point eight pounds. He's making his New Breed debut. [He] fights out of Advanced Martial Arts. Let's hear it for Dave Greeeeeennbeeerrrrrrrg!!!" The crowd erupts in cheers as my walkout music gets blasted through the speakers.

Now that might not look like much, especially if you can't read sheet music. But that is the drum intro to Disturbed's "Down with the Sickness," and there are few if any harmonized sounds that got me up like this one.

Can you feel that?
Ah, shit
Oh, ah, ah, ah, ah
Oh, ah, ah, ah, ah
oh, oh, oh, oh, oh, oh
Drowning deep in my sea of loathing
Broken your servant I kneel
(Will you give in to me?)
It seems what's left of my human side
Is slowly changing in me
(Will you give in to me?)
Looking at my own reflection
When suddenly it changes
Violently it changes (oh no)
There is no turning back now

You've woken up the demon in me
Get up, come on get down with the sickness
Get up, come on get down with the sickness
Get up, come on get down with the sickness…

Now I don't fully resonate with all of the lyrics, but a transformation had begun before battle. The demon within had been summoned.

That music was my, Max's, and Brian's cue to start my walk out to the cage. We emerged from the dank stairwell to be led by one of the ring card girls to the cage.

"Dude check out her ass," Brian suggested to me.

"*Dude,* I'm focused on an imminent cage fight."

"Oh right. Well it's nice."

My liberated beast snarled inwardly, harnessing that added rage for all of Brian's lack of focus this whole time. My relatively small entourage and I walked down the arena stairs past the crowded rows of spectators. Though my entourage was small, it was made up for by my fierce and numerous supporters.

My fans were screaming my nickname.

"MEANBERG! MEANBERG! MEANBERG!"

I was aware of them, but only peripherally. I would not make eye contact as I descended down the spaced-out stairs to the beat of the music, and I had a lightness in my cadence on my way to the cage. I donned my warrior face, cool and steeled, ready for the task at hand. They screamed louder as I passed, but I would not break my laser focus. I hit the stairs to the stage leading to the cage just as the song hit a vocal climax.

"OOOH, AAHHH, AAHHH, AAHHH, AAHHH!"

I ran up the stairs on that beat.

The crowd did not let up—their roars intensified as the two adjacent big screens on either side of the cage zoomed in on me as I started to receive directives from one of the referees. I was directed by the ref to give my shirt to my trainer and cornerman and to embrace them. I handed Brian my shirt, slapped him a high five, gave him a quick bro hug, and then did the same with Max. Brian then prepared me for war by placing Vaseline on the ridge of my eyebrows and nose, and my cheekbones to help prevent cuts by having my opponent's strikes slide off their intended target—my face. It was the first time I had been prepped in this way. It felt like I was having my war paint applied. When Brian finished, he gave me an encouraging pat on the back before handing me back over to the referee. The ref asked, "Do you have your mouthpiece in?" I flashed my teeth, baring my mouth guard. He instructed me to extend my arms out sideward and began inspecting to see if I was greased. He felt behind my ears, my neck, my shoulders, and both my arms. "All good there. Are you wearing your cup?" I nodded and knocked on the cup a couple of times. And with that he stepped aside, extended his arm to point to the cage entrance, permitting me to enter. The announcer came back over the loudspeaker. He was barely louder than the screaming crowd, announcing me again as I entered the cage, "DAAAVE GREEEEEENBERRRG!!!"

I broke into a jog as I ascended the final stairs into the cage. As my foot touched the soft canvas, I was transported back to the night before—I had been here before. I was ready to do what needed to be done. I continued the rehearsed ritual and instantly side-shuffled around the perimeter of the cage. After only one revolution, I was corralled by a different ref in the cage and directed to the blue corner, my corner.

The announcer started in on my opponent's introduction, and I returned to my rhythmic bouncing to keep warm and showcase my athleticism that I worked so hard to attain, or maybe I was just buoying myself. My disproportionately large group of supporters changed their cheers to boos. This embarrassed me some, but I did appreciate the support, and heck, they had been drinking. When Borders made it cage side to go through the same inspection from the referee was when I got my first glimpse of him since entering the arena. Instincts were starting to take over. I was laying eyes on my enemy, at least for the next 11 minutes (give or take). Instinct had it so that I began gnawing at my mouthpiece—chomping at the bit again.

There was a touch of madness one had to let in, so that our inner savagery could be levied for our own safety when in a combat situation such as this. For all practical purposes, I was treating my opponent as someone ready and willing to kill me. *Not on my watch*. My body was priming itself and signaling it was not a good idea to threaten my existence. Thank God that it is rare, but people have died in the cage fighting. It sure was something to have had months to contemplate what being locked in a cage with a trained killer might have felt like. It was far more intense than I could have imagined—than anyone could imagine—until having it done it. Heightened fear kept me sharp. I was simultaneously confident in my training and anxious for the impending chaos.

I thrived in chaos though. Borders stepped into the cage, and although I was not a very religious man, I said a prayer.

"Please God, look over my opponent and I so that neither one of us gets seriously hurt."

Twenty-nine

Are You Ready?

Pomp and circumstance were over and done with. Now was time for battle. Borders stepped into the cage. The cage door closed behind him, and the latch locked. *I hope you know what you're doing*. The referee summoned us to the middle for final instructions.

"Protect yourself at all times. Obey my commands at all

times. Any questions?"

We both shake our heads.

"OK. Let's have a good, clean fight. Touch gloves and come out fighting."

We obliged and returned to our designated corners. I began bouncing on the balls of my feet. The ref pointed to me.

"Ready?"

I nodded.

"Get your hands up."

Holy Crap he's right, I thought and quickly got my hands up.

He pointed to Borders. "Ready?"

Borders nodded with his hands by his waist as well and received the same command.

"Get your hands up."

Ding. Here we go.

Sometimes fights begin with another touching of the gloves to further signify sportsmanship, but the look in Borders' eyes made it clear that that was not his intention. While I might have preferred to start with that symbolic gesture, I wasn't going to ask for it when he was busy mean mugging and looking through me. *You want a fist fight? I'll give you a fist fight.*

We met in the middle and circled each other for just a second. Borders opened with a pawing jab and a power right hook behind it. I beat him to the punch with a straight right, which connected to his face. I threw a pawing jab of my own, and Borders slipped (ducked under it), reloaded, and countered with another power right hook, this one connecting half on the side of my jaw and half on my neck. He followed up throwing wildly with more hooks from both left and right hands. I ducked them and initiated a clinch to push him back against the cage. (A clinch is the part of stand-up fighting when a combatant secures a controlling hold. Clinching an opponent can be used to limit the opponent's ability to kick and punch, or to transition from stand-up fighting to ground fighting by using takedowns, throws or sweeps). As we careened towards the cage, I had my left hand holding the back of his head as I threw a right uppercut, employing a bit of dirty boxing (while dirty boxing sounds dastardly, it's a perfectly legal MMA technique). Borders responded with a knee to my ribs, creating enough space for him to land a 3-4-3 combination (lead side hook, reverse side hook, lead side hook) to my chin, temple, and back to my chin. After landing his combination, we separated and circled back to the center. This time I opened. I attempted a 1-2 combination (lead-side jab, reverse-side straight punch), but Borders bobbed and weaved successfully and returned fire with a counter straight right. I blocked the counter and took a stab at initiating another clinch as I pushed him back to the cage. As Borders retreated, he threw a power right hook that glanced off the side of my head. He pushed me off, set his feet, and threw a feeler left jab and power straight right that directly impacted, snapping my head back violently. I felt something give in my neck, immediately followed by a sharp searing pain in the same place. It was years later when I went to the doctor for numbness and tingling down my left arm that an MRI revealed an old acute injury of a herniated disc in my neck. Upon the doctor reading the scan, I was instantly brought back to this punch, which snapped my head back. It was only twenty seconds into the fight when I suffered that herniated disc in my neck and fought through it. Thankfully I kept my poker face in that moment, and Borders circled off back to the center.

That's not good. Maybe try some of your kicks. I feinted a leg kick to see how Borders reacted. Nothing. Still timing him, I waited a moment or two and threw the same kick, landing it this time, but Borders was ready for it. He immediately countered with a straight right hand that had some seriously bad intentions behind it. I got lucky as I was not in a position to deal with it properly, and that piston of a straight right only grazed me. That punch had so much steam behind it that had it fully connected, in all probability it would have put me out. Instinctually I went to initiate the clinch yet again, but Borders was savvy to it and pushed away before I could garner control. As we reset, I reflected that I had gotten away with one there.

We continued to circle one another, still trying to time the other. Borders threw a four-punch combination (1-2-1-2) as he advanced. I retreated and effectively parried and blocked the incoming fire. *OK, he's getting the better of me in the boxing. Attempting my kicking techniques almost got me knocked out. Next combination he throws, look to take him down.* Borders feigned a punch, and I all too eagerly took the bait. Out of position, from too far away, I committed to a sloppy double-leg takedown attempt. I lowered my level, skipped a proper penetration step, and more or less dove at Borders' legs. Borders easily evaded by sprawling, and he simultaneously locked up an arm in guillotine chokehold. I quickly popped to my feet, but Borders was able to maintain his dominant chokehold, and he began to push me full force into the cage. I focused on defending the choke and was relatively pleased he elected to push me to the cage instead of concentrating on finishing the choke. I allowed him to push me towards the cage and at the last instant, I switched my hips and threw him into the cage while I was still caught in the choke. Borders was content enough with the choke that he didn't fight himself off the cage. I had been here before; I had trained this position countless times, and I knew how to defend. I continued to fight his grip, preventing him from finishing the choke as I paid careful attention that he didn't try to throw any knees in my compromised position. While successfully defending the choke, I couldn't break free completely. With one hand fighting his grip, I used my free hand to start throwing uppercuts to his body in the hopes to soften him up some and have him focus on defending the strikes to distract him from his hold on me. Instead, he tried to readjust his grip to a traditional guillotine choke to finish the submission, but I sensed the moment he attempted to do so and almost broke free. He again grabbed hold of the choke with my arm in, and I started to take him down from this position. He reacted by squeezing tighter as my hands were now no longer defending the choke and instead were being used to take him down. I gave up the takedown attempt to defend being choked again. I threw one more uppercut to his body, creating an angle, and popped my head free from his grasp.

We circled to the center again. *Shit man, this is going to be a long night.* I was getting my ass kicked on our feet, and my takedown attempts were effortlessly thwarted. Borders attempted a long-range punch that I easily avoided. I then attempted an equally long-range punch that he too easily dodged in turn. I sensed Borders' confidence growing from our exchanges. He was stalking now, walking me down. He feinted a punch; I reacted. I feinted a punch; he reacted. Borders then changed his timing. Leaping forward, pushing hard off his back foot, he led with a straight right hand that connected and snapped my head back again. He narrowly missed the left hook behind it, not for any evasive action on my part. I was in survival mode at this point and grabbed a hold of him to clinch and control again, but we were both so sweaty and slippery that Borders was able to push off and wriggle free with no trouble. I was hurt from that punch and couldn't sustain another shot like that, not at least until the cobwebs cleared out. As he retreated to establish striking distance, I recklessly charged in to try and regain control through grappling holds. Despite moving backward, Borders was able to load up on a power right hand. He launched it, and with perfect accuracy, it hit its mark right on my chin, amidst all of the chaos. The punch was so brutal that it violently shook my head side to side three times in a split second.

Getting hit directly on the chin is often referred to as getting hit on the "button" as in "the off button." You can probably guess that it got its name because when that button is hit, consciousness turns off as a result. The number of variables (velocity of the punch, force at impact, speed of the ensuing deceleration, personal anatomy, etc.) will determine the duration of being knocked unconscious, and it can range from being knocked down to being knocked out cold. In boxing, if one is knocked down, the competition halts and the downed opponent has 10 seconds to try and rouse and recover before continuing. In MMA there is no break in the action. There is no 10 count. If the fighter cannot intelligently defend themselves, the fight is over.

As you know by now, I was separated from my consciousness. I woke up as I was crashing down to the canvas. Understanding I had been dropped with the awareness there would be no break in the action, I kept fighting. I took no break. Good thing too because Borders had thrown another punch with bad intentions, which just narrowly missed me and surely would have ended my night. As soon as my hands hit the canvas, I sprung to my feet and simultaneously shot in for a takedown. I slammed Borders into the cage with my shot attempt, and we found ourselves in a similar position from the one earlier in the round where Borders secured another arm in a guillotine choke. He pulled up on it and squeezed to complete the submission, and I pressured hard into him against the cage. *It's not ideal to take him down while caught in the choke, but I can't risk taking another shot like I just had. This fight has to go to the ground. I must take him down.* There was no contingency; I poured all of my effort wholeheartedly to that one task. I would not be denied.

It wasn't technical, and it definitely wasn't pretty, but I muscled Borders down to the ground. Due to taking Borders down wildly, he was able to sink the choke deeper. Out of the frying pan and into the fire. This choke was deeper than anything I had been caught in for all of my training leading up to the fight. Additionally, I was entirely spent from the fight to this point: the adrenaline dump, getting dropped, and forcing the takedown. I had nothing left in the tank. Borders may have sensed that I was close to the end and went all out to try and finish the submission. I employed the strategy of what was affectionately known in some jiu-jitsu circles as letting your opponent "blow their wad." The idea was to let Borders fully exhaust his energy in trying to finish the fight and to simply outlast him. It didn't work. My world began greying out. The next phase was being choked unconscious. I reached to begin fighting his grip, and Borders accurately took that as a sign that I was close to being finished and squeezed harder. I flailed and bucked wildly to desperately create some space. He squeezed harder still. I had just about all I could take. That evil quiet thought crept into my mind.

You can just tap out and this will all be over.

That voice telling me to quit had more force behind it given my exhausted and battered state. I was at my limit; I had taken a beating everywhere this fight had gone.

What are you even holding out for. Say you break free—is it better to get knocked out after exerting all this effort?

The voice had grown stronger. I came as close as possible to giving in and tapping out when the cheers and pleas of the crowd broke through that evil voice's monopoly of my attention. They were screaming for me to break free, and I was trying, but it wasn't working. In that moment, I decided I couldn't give up. I wasn't sure I would be able to escape, but I couldn't give up after dragging all of these supporters here to quit before them. I silenced that evil voice and gave into my fate, whatever it should be, trying my best.

I can't quit. If I get choked unconscious so be it, but I won't quit.

That very next moment, Borders fatigued and loosened his grip infinitesimally, but loosened nonetheless. Like trying to fight a Chinese finger trap, pulling against the force was making it tighter, and with that realization, I went with it, and in the direction of making the choke deeper—instantly giving me more room to breathe and catch my breath. Interestingly that insidious voice didn't leave as easily at it came. I had to continue my inner dialogue with myself.

This still sucks. You're still exhausted and outclassed in all facets of this contest. You're still caught in the choke. You can still tap.

Oddly, my inner critic knew just the right language to use. Had he said I could still quit, I would have pushed against that. Tap seems more innocuous; it chose that word purposefully. In an attempt to convince myself more than battle that inner detractor I asked myself, *Why would I need to tap if I can breathe? Besides I already decided I'm not tapping. If he puts me out, he puts me out.* And like a wizard uttering the right spell, that inner demon was vanquished for the remainder of the fight.

Resting and catching my breath was a double-edged sword as it allowed Borders to do the same, and he still had the upper hand. This is where all my hard work of hill sprints and long runs began to pay off. I recovered slightly more quickly. There was that saying in the MMA community that each blow you took to the dome knocked a stripe off your belt. In one swift move I explosively, inarticulately muscled my way out of the hold like a determined white belt without any stripes on that belt. I ended up in his guard, a much more neutral position than the one I was just caught in. Borders tried to match my intensity by ramping up his effort to keep me in the hold, but all those miles I had run made it so I was just barely able to escape. Imagine I had run one less mile or one less hill sprint. That explosive action we each took (me to escape, him to try and hold on) re-exhausted the both of us, and we began to rest to catch our breaths again. There was an internal clock going off in my mind at this point. If this inactivity persisted, the referee would stand us up to force more action. I threw a couple of weak punches to Borders ribs (as the rules precluded me from striking to his head) to hopefully satisfy the ref as I continued to catch my breath. I caught my breath more quickly than Borders again. A pattern was emerging. I used that found energy to posture up and deliver one power shot to his solar plexus, thinking finally it was my time to try and win back the round. Just then, Borders caught his wind and threw up an armbar submission attempt. I reacted, defended, and took advantage of his opening up, by advancing my position. I finally achieved my first dominant position of the fight, and it was time to go to work. *Ding!*

Thirty

From Where You Least Expect It

The referee stepped in to disentangle us. I staggered to my feet and stumbled back to my corner. There waiting for me was Max in his dress clothes, accented with latex surgical gloves and a towel around his neck, and of course my oh so reassuring trainer Brian. I needn't remind you that Brian didn't believe I was ready for this fight. By all accounts of what had just happened—he was right not to believe in me. He knew something I didn't. He knew better. I braced for Brian's justified chastising, "I told you so," or "This is what you get," or "Careful what you wish for."

Instead, Brian bellowed, "Sit down! Shut up! You're gonna win this thing!"

"Dude are you crazy?! What do you mean I'm 'gonna win this thing?' Did you even see what happened out there?! I got my ass kicked everywhere the fight went! I was dropped on my feet and almost choked out on the ground!" (Not to mention the herniated disc in my neck I didn't know I had)

"You know you can take him down now. Don't force it. Pick your spot and take him back down."

Max opened a bottle of water and handed it to Brian. "Here drink this."

"Nah, I don't need it."

"Just drink it."

I was extremely gassed from that round and was sucking some serious air. I took one swig and realized I wasn't going to be able to swallow it down. I looked for the bucket to spit in, and it was nowhere to be found. I started to get desperate for my next gulp of air, and even though I knew better—I didn't care. I spit it out all over the canvas. I reasoned—*What are they going to do punish me? Stop the fight because I spit water on the ground? Unlikely.* Either way, I had to do it. The auxiliary ref assigned to my corner freaked out.

"You can't do that!" he hollered.

Good luck getting that toothpaste back in the tube, I half-laughed to myself.

"MOP IT NOW!" he screamed at Max.

Poor Max got down on his hands and knees in dress clothes to wipe it up the best he could with that towel that was wrapped around his neck.

The head referee started to impatiently clap his hands and commanded, "Let's go! Let's go! Let's go!" All of that water drama took up almost the entire minute between rounds. I stood up from the stool and took a deep breath. *Here we go again.* "Look for the takedown," Brian called out as he exited the cage.

Thirty-one

(In) The Zone

As the referee tended to some housekeeping issues (making sure the cage doors were properly secured and that the judges were ready for the round to start), Borders took to the center of the cage and started pacing like a lion at feeding time, presumably ready to resume the mauling from the first round. The referee turned back around to see Borders in the center and directed him back to his corner. Then he turned to me and reminded me again:

"Get your hands up."

Right! I quickly oblige.

Ding!

Click. I snapped into a state where I was no longer in my head thinking. In the first round, I had been consumed with thoughts like, *If Borders does X, I do Y, etc.* I wasn't in my head anymore. I was in the present moment. Without preconceptions, I was better able to just be and express myself in the present. I snapped into my default self.

We met in the middle, and then my stance took more of a karate form for the first time in the fight, and I let it all flow. Borders advanced, and I was bouncing on the balls of my feet. I sprung backward, maintaining karate distance. Borders methodically stalked me as he continued to march forward. Still maintaining the distance, I was more natural, but I stayed primed, ready to strike. I feinted a lead right hand measuring Borders reaction the whole time. He jumped backward, then realized it was only a feint and resumed his forward pressure. I saw an opening and acted immediately, launching a fully committed leg kick accompanied with a robust Kiai (battle scream used in the Asian martial arts). While Bruce Lee's Kiai would shame mine, employing the technique signified my return to my roots of the first traditional martial art I had studied.

I feinted another leg kick with a Kiai, and Borders reacted and retreated immediately. Clearly getting frustrated with the new look I was presenting, he initiated some of his own offense. He loaded up, and leaped forward, throwing a lead right-hand power shot. No longer in my head, I reacted with more entrenched muscle memory from traditional karate—an old-school block. I circled off like a matador, and Borders acted like a compliant bull and went careening all the way to the cage from the center of the canvas.

Borders walked back to the center of the cage to meet me, still in his stalking cadence. Frustrated that I was able to send him flying with his own momentum, he led with another right hand without hesitation. I initiated the same block, but it was a slightly wrong read as Borders made a slight adjustment himself and straightened the punch out. As a result, he connected, landing the end of his punch square on my nose, and my head jerked back once again. Maintaining my karate distance prevented the punch landing with more force, and my block wasn't completely ineffectual as it was able to deflect some of the force as well. I regrouped quickly, and now it was Borders circling me from the outside. I was controlling the center; it was now my cage, and I changed the pace. No feint, I executed and landed another leg kick on his lead leg. Borders started to feel the effects of those kicks and switched stances to protect that lead leg. He circled me some more and returned to his default traditional stance. More tentative now that I had earned some more of his respect, he opened again, but thought better of over-committing with an opening power shot and threw a jab. Time began to slow for me, and my own timing was getting sharper. I blocked his jab and ripped another leg kick, slamming my shinbone into the meaty part of his inner thigh. With his frustration rising, he pushed me to create space, but having my center under me, it was he that stumbled backward for his effort. It was still my cage.

Stymied thus far in this round with his singular shots, Borders shifted gears and threw his first combination of the round with a 1-2. I thwarted both, still finding success with my blocking techniques. His offense temporarily knocked me from my center control, but it was now me exercising a stalking gait, and I simply walked him out from the center, rightfully reclaiming it. Frustration mounting, Borders blitzed in with another combination 1-2-3-2. I slipped the first two punches, blocked the third, and Borders misfired the last one in the frenzy, glancing off my body. I sensed my moment and went to commence a clinch. Borders instantly reacted like he did in the first round, attempting to push me off. Being in the flow state, my body took over without thought. I pursued his retreat all the way to the cage, slamming him into it. I anticipated his rebounding body from the springiness of the cage and timed a level change by attacking his legs, shooting in on a double-leg down takedown. Unable to sprawl because the cage was in the way, Borders grabbed a body lock, and I lifted him off his feet, cutting the corner (finding an angle for leverage), and slamming him to the canvas. Borders tried to establish his guard (controlling one's opponent between your legs), but I secured the dominant position of side control by passing his legs and disallowing him to regain position.

It was finally time for me to put in some real work from this dominant position. Trouble was, under the amateur rules set, I was disallowed to strike Borders' head now that the fight was on the ground. Additionally, with the fight sufficiently underway, both of us were sweaty enough that going for a submission would likely result in giving up my hard-fought dominant position. I decided it was best to control my opponent and punish his body—scoring points on the judges' scorecards and hopefully depleting his endurance reserves. Brian was calling from the corner for me to advance my position.

"Right knee on his belly! Dave! Right knee on his

belly!"

Technically I knew Brian was right in his instruction, but I was valuing controlling Borders over advancing my position. Again, I thought attempting a submission was too risky to my dominant position, and Brian's guidance for me to advance I deemed would be more valuable if I were allowed to strike to Border's head from that position.

Brian was incessant. "DAVE! RIGHT KNEE ON HIS BELLY!"

I wasn't exactly in a position where I could have a whole dialogue with Brian to share my chain of reasoning, but I did want him to know I heard him, so between punches to Borders' midsection, I signaled to Brian the international sign of "one minute" by raising my index finger to him.

Borders powerfully attempted to restore his guard. I kept calm, and the muscle memory of my drilled technique allowed me to block his hips and circle to his head, maintaining my dominant position and tiring him out all the while. I loaded up and delivered a power shot to his gut to reward his effort. Borders mustn't have liked it, as he dug deeper and exploded more fiercely this time, restoring his guard. He then prematurely attempted a triangle choke (choke administered by the legs blocking blood flow through the carotid arteries by forcing one's opponent's own arm against their neck), but he hadn't properly secured his guard back, which allowed me to catch his legs, throw them aside, and pass his guard right back. Now, ticked off that Borders should have the audacity to fight for position in a fight, I raised my fist high above my head and slammed a hammer fist right to his soft underbelly. I could feel the energy leaving his body with that landed strike. That'll learn him.

Or so I thought. Turns out he didn't like that too much either, and he wasn't going to layover for me. He harnessed his new-found motivation to explode for a third time. This time, it wasn't to return guard. He had secured an underhook, allowing him enough space to blast upward to his feet. I was caught off guard he had the energy and ability to do that given how easily I had thwarted his other attempts. Off balance, but with instincts still firing on all cylinders, I attempted to secure a guillotine choke as I was falling backward. Borders deftly took advantage of my imbalance and crashed me into the cage. Wanting immediate payback for my hammer fist, he hurled a heavy right-hand power shot straight for my dome that narrowly missed. I gave up the choke attempt and settled for establishing a clinch. With the clinch properly procured, I used it to maneuver Borders against the cage. With my left hand securely grasping the back of his head, I freed my right hand to deliver a quick punch to the side of his head. This may have been a mistake as there was no power behind it, and it awoke Borders to the possibility of returning fire with his own right hand. Only he was savvy enough to use his left to push off my face, creating distance as he loaded up for yet another power shot that landed square on the side of my head. Well, I didn't like that one bit and responded with what I was establishing as my own dominance. I lowered my level, shot a hard, double-leg takedown, slamming into the cage and using his momentum with his recoil off of it to thwack him back to the canvas with a thud. I was rewarded with the same choke I had been caught in in the first round that had me come close to tapping out. The difference this time was that I hadn't just been severed from my consciousness moments before, and sensed the choke as it was being applied. I defended and broke free from the choke much more quickly this time. And now it was my time again to deliver more punishment. Borders wasn't waiting around. Before I could dispense any of my offense, he threw up an armbar submission attempt with the aim of breaking my arm at the elbow via hyperextension. I swiftly defended, and keener on punishing his efforts, loaded up a power right hand. I let it fly. Trouble was, it was launched with the authority of a heat-seeking missile, and his head was the target. I realized mid punch I had initiated an illegal strike, and at the last minute, using all of my energy, I was barely able to redirect the punch to his shoulder instead.

Still in the same position, Borders threw up another armbar attempt, and I quickly utilized the opportunity again. Without ever having a conversation, Brian realized my strategy, and in place of calling for me to advance positions, he called for me to take a greater position of control. "North-south! Go north-south!" The position north-south holds pretty true to its namesake. It is a move where my upper body would still be controlling Borders' upper body, but our legs would be outstretched opposite from one another like the poles. Though it wasn't part of my plan, I trusted my trainer because I would like to avoid Borders' escaping again, so I keenly obliged. With Borders properly immobilized, I begin ripping punches to his gut and his ribs. Like the climactic fistfight scenes of the Batman television series in the late 1960s, punctuated with onomatopoeias superimposed with bright colors over the action, mimicking the comic books, I land eight unanswered punches:

BAM! KAPOW! WHAMM! ZAP! BLAP! SOK! BIFF! POW!

Borders had enough, dug deep, and grabbed an awkward headlock and rolled with it, off balancing me and enabling him to make it back to his feet.

Back on our feet, I rapidly rushed in going for the clinch again as Borders tried to land one of his signature power punches. Borders whiffed on the punch, and I whiffed on the clinch. Excuse me, I mean:

WHIFF! WHIFF!

The resulting position of both our misses was me falling into the cage face first with Borders behind in the process of securing my back (one of the most dominant positions in all of martial arts). It took me less than a split second to react as I was not keen on giving up my back. I turned to face him as I used the cage as a tool to literally scrape Borders from my back. In a slightly better position than I had been in before, it still wasn't perfect—Borders was now pinning my back against the cage. I instinctively threatened with a guillotine choke, and Borders took it upon himself to land a power knee right to my belly!

SLOG!

OK last cheesy onomatopoeia.

I winced in pain as the wind literally got knocked out of me. I raised my own knee in a defensive posture to protect my fragile midsection from what I believed to be another incoming knee. Instead though, Borders pushed me off to create space and started landing power punches again. I instinctively went to block, but my reflexes were too quick this time, and Borders observed my attempted block and waited a split second before launching his next punch. Lucky for me he missed, and I marched forward under fire to grab that clinch hold. I attained it, but Borders landed another power shot to my skull for my effort. Now pinning Borders against the cage, I had my clinch that I had strived and paid for, and used to it hurl a knee strike of my own. Thing was, Borders was savvy to it and easily blocked the strike. He could also hear my corner calling for more knees and responded by maintaining that framed-out position of his arms to block any more knees I may have launched. I threw a fake knee to see how he would react and he committed to blocking it. I faked one more, and as Borders went to block the feigned knee strike, I ducked under for a quick double-leg takedown, returning him to the mat.

This takedown landed me in Borders' guard. He quickly wrapped me up to prevent me raining down strikes from that top position. Unlucky for Borders though, I had one hand free and was able to hit his ribs four times consecutively in the same spot, getting him to open up a little and allowing me to start to work my head and other arm out from his hold. Timed perfectly with popping my head out, Borders went for *another* armbar. I defended with relative ease. Borders made the mistake of rolling to his belly, and my eyes widened like saucers. I saw an opportunity to end the fight with a rear naked choke—one of the most effective techniques from one of the most dominant positions. I pounced full force. Borders, in recognizing his vulnerability, promptly rolled to his back and prevented me from sinking in the choke. His maneuver was so fast and unexpected that my own hastened movement to secure the choke from his previous fixed point didn't give me time enough to adjust. I inadvertently struck him across the forehead, opening up a gash across it. We were both unaware and continued our fight for position. Unable to secure the back mount, I achieved the second most dominant position: traditional mount (sitting on Borders stomach, passed his legs). I immediately went for an Ezekiel choke from the mount (low percentage, but low risk of giving up position). I locked it on and started to apply pressure, when *Ding!*

Thirty-two

Just Breathe

The round ended with Borders and me right by my corner. I got to my feet and was able to sit down on the stool without so much as taking a step. My lungs were burning, and it was safe to say this was the most exhausted I had ever felt. As I was doing my best to catch my breath and bring my heart rate down, I had a prime view of Borders lackadaisically making his way back to his corner. His corner, however, had the opposite mindset. They were insisting Borders move more quickly to attend to the laceration I had opened across his forehead.

Meanwhile, my own corner was doing their best to

wash Borders' blood off my chest. It had gotten there when I went to sink in the choke at the very end of the round. I think I was equally oblivious to the blood as Borders was. My attention was being stolen by the stinging pain in my lungs. I was rocking back and forth—I think in retrospect to take my mind off the pain. I leaned forward, resting my elbows on my knees just to not have to carry the weight of my upper body. Brian, while holding ice on the back of my neck, pushed me upright. Conventional wisdom said sitting tall and upright allowed for more air to enter the lungs, but I resisted, as it felt worse to sit up straight and collapsed my upper body back down.

I'm sure Brian was offering me sage advice, but I couldn't process any of it. I was just too tired and in too much pain. *How am I going to fight another whole round?*

Wheeeuw! The whistle blew for the trainers to get out of the cage. I stood facing the task ahead. All of the doubt fled my mind as did the pain in my lungs. *Let's get this!*

Thirty-three

Third and Final Round

Borders stood up and began pacing back and forth again. However, he did not claim the center like he had previously. I was conserving my energy, waiting for the ref's instruction to commence.

The ref pointed to Borders. "Are you ready?"

He nodded.

The ref pointed to me. "Are you ready?"

I nodded.

I remembered to put my hands up, and after doing so, the ref reminded me anyway.

"Get your hands up."

They're up, dude. Let's go.

"Fight!"

I plodded forward to stake ownership of the center of the cage. Borders obliged and circled me from the outside. Without telegraphing, he blitzed forward initiating a combination (1-2). He intended to throw more, but I countered by sliding back and circling off as I threw a defensive jab. Borders regrouped and fired back with a jab of his own that I slipped. Next, we then both threw punches at the same time. He threw and landed a cross that beat my overloaded, overhand right to the mark, stunning me. With my momentum already going forward from overcommitting to my power shot, I transitioned to a double-leg takedown shot. Borders sprawled and stalled my shot. I adjusted mid-shot, gained an underhook, and initiated a poorly formed hip toss from my knees. To my utter surprise, it worked enough to off-balance him and allowed me to follow through by raising my hips up—effectively throwing Borders through the air. He crashed to the mat, and I swiftly seized control.

Exhausted, I resigned myself to Borders' guard. Fearing that the referee may stand us back up for inactivity, I began throwing half-powered punches to Borders ribs as I tried to regain my breath. I realized my best odds were when I was controlling him on the ground. Borders was better than me on our feet (at least with the amateur rules, disallowing me to kick him in the head). Even though the shots I was throwing were only half-powered, five of them to the same point on his ribs added up, and Borders responded by setting up for a kimura (attack on the shoulder joint to separate or dislocate). I recognized his intention and defended by posturing up and freeing my arm. Borders reached up and grabbed behind my head to break my posture and deny me space. I braced, holding my posture, and Borders elected to let go to conserve his own energy. With a little bit more wind in my lungs, I resumed my offense. I sat back and began to dig the points of my elbows into Borders' inner thighs as a way to get him to open his guard. Borders tried to resist and realized pretty early on that he wouldn't be able to and quickly transitioned into a sweep attempt (reversing from the bottom to top position). I kept my balance and paid him back by pinning him back down to the canvas, as I landed a quick sharp punch to his gut. Immediately after, I loaded to deliver a power shot to really make him pay for trying to overthrow my hard-fought position. Borders saw it coming and with both hands, tried to intercept. From a locked and loaded position, I made minute adjustments, seeking an opening. Realizing he was so focused on my right, I threw my left instead. Without quite as much dexterity as my right hand, my left hand sailed wide, missing the mark. Borders capitalized by reaching up, grabbing hold of me, and breaking my posture, denying me the room to deliver devastating blows. I adjusted and threw four more shots to that same point on his ribs I had moments before—only this time with full power. Borders understandably didn't like that and grasped my right hand to halt the onslaught. Borders, overcommitting to my right, allowed me to deliver two power shots to his other set of ribs with my left. He then was forced to focus on that and grabbed my left to stop the pummeling. Like a dance, I transitioned. Now that he was holding my left hand, I delivered two more power shots to his ribs with my right. Having just about all the punishment his ribs could take, Borders tried to initiate a high guard—something that would control my posture better and allow him to more easily set up an armbar or a triangle choke. I shucked off the attempt and postured all the way back up. I threw a wild right hand and just barely grazed him with it. Borders started to feel the full effects of fatigue and slumped backward with both of his arms outstretched over his head. I used my left hand as a combination range finder and immobilizer by holding his neck and delivered another power shot to his underbelly. Borders, frustrated, sat up to break my posture again. I reinforced my framed left arm, holding him by the throat and threw him back down to the canvas. On the way back down, I reached high over my head and slugged yet another powerful shot right into his fatiguing body. Borders couldn't take many more of those shots and responded by throwing up another triangle submission. I easily and immediately defended and passed his guard. I was on my way to the north-south position.

With far more control, I landed two more punches to that same point on his ribs. Desperate not to take any more punishment there, Borders, with more energy than I thought he had, tried to regain guard by creating distance and began circling. I gave up my offense to maintain my position and circled right along with him. We rotated a full 360 degrees, which may not sound like much, but you try that with an opponent on top of you in the last round of a grueling fight.

After we completed our rotation and ended up right back where we started, I could feel Borders' will deflating seemingly in sync with his collapsing framed-out arms. I had Borders in a spot where I feared most I might end up—in a subordinate position with less energy than me. Now pinning him to the canvas with all of my weight on top, embolizing him, I was free to wind and load up like I hadn't been before. Digging in deep and hitting harder than even my power shots to his ribs, I landed six thudding punches right to the softest most vulnerable part of Borders' body. I sensed this might be the end. If I were allowed to strike his head on the ground, this surely would have been the end. Just as I thought Borders might give in, I heard his corner cry out with real desperation in his voice, "GET OUT OF THERE!"

Borders responded like a heart-attack victim getting shocked back to life with a defibrillator, and bucked violently, enabling him to roll over to his stomach and then up to his knees. He exposed his neck in the process, and I executed a guillotine submission attempt. Borders aptly fought off my grip and sprung to his feet in one fell swoop.

Eager to bring the fight back to where I was dominant, as soon as we were both upright, I shot in to take him right back down. Only, I slipped on the attempt as Borders sprawled, slamming my face directly into the canvas with all of his weight. I still tried to finish the takedown from my compromised position, but Borders properly stretched his leg back, causing my loose grip on it to crash to the mat. For the first time in the fight, Borders had dominant top positioning over me. I imagined he would probably remember what I had done to him when I had top position, and that he was all too eager to return the favor. I kept my cool despite feeling oh so vulnerable. Borders began to advance his position by spinning and tried to take my back. Just then the strangest thing happened: my muscle memory kicked in in a way I never experienced. One of the new moves I had learned in that last-minute BJJ seminar must have sunk into my nervous system before my psyche. As Borders went to advance, I slipped right into that newly learned deep half-guard position (think of it as when you're a kid and your dad comes home from work and you latch onto his leg with all four limbs). Using that I was able to continue with Borders own momentum and roll through. Rolling through created just enough space for me to start to get my feet. Still on the ground, Borders threw a strike that connected with the side of my head (technically an illegal strike, but this a fight and everything is happening so fast. That, and I had accidentally already delivered him one illegal blow the round before). I still managed to get to my feet, but Borders slapped on another guillotine hold for my effort. I took a tiny step backward towards the cage. Borders obliged and took an equally tiny step forward to fill the gap. We repeated that dance step seven more times still with a firm grasp around my neck. That seventh step got us back to the cage, and on my eighth step, instead of taking a backward step, I took a side step, starting to circle

Borders' back against the cage. Perhaps because he had a dominant position, he obliged and took a baby circle step bringing him that much closer the cage. We did that a couple more times and with Borders back sufficiently up against the cage, I elected to pop my head out. Turns out Borders must have been plotting for me to free myself in that way the whole time. Like a kid at Chuck-E-Cheese playing whack-a-mole who had figured out the pattern of where that mole would be, Borders wound up and unleashed a full-power shot, landing squarely on the side of my head. He tried to follow with a left hook, but I already rushed in to pin him to the cage, and that hook actually missed its mark by swinging wide behind my head. Having enough of that, I shot in for another double-leg takedown. Thankfully I didn't slip on this one and completed the bid.

Totally exhausted again (in part from getting cracked upside the head) I crumbled inside of Borders guard. Fearing a standup from the referee, I threw three hammer fists that were so lacking in power your grandmother could have thrown harder. Borders' was sensing that it was me that was exhausted now, and set up another armbar, but quickly released the hold, realizing that he too was exhausted. I threw a few more of those ineffectual punches with lungs burning ferociously all the while. Borders began to squirm, and as tired as he was, I could feel he had more energy than I. In attempt to zap some of that energy and stop his squirming I covered his mouth to disrupt his breathing. Borders didn't like that one bit and responded by grabbing hold of both of my arms. I was so tired that I let him have them.

After enough time elapsed, I regained enough liveliness to posture up and deliver another punch to Borders' midsection. Borders not wanting to play that game whatsoever, threw up a triangle submission. I easily defended and transitioned to passing his guard. The position we found ourselves in was between side control and north-south. The cage itself was preventing me from achieving the north-south position. Borders' head was pressed up against the cage, as well as my back. I had one arm controlling his body, and with my free hand, I landed thirteen unanswered shots to that same point on his ribs. Borders' corner got desperate again and pleaded for him to, "GET OUT OF THERE!"

Borders found the strength again to explode out from underneath the punishment I was delivering. I tried to grab a hold of his neck and missed.

Back on our feet, I went for the clinch and Borders landed another power shot on my head. I charged forward still fighting for the clinch. Borders pushed off me, took a step back, and landed an even harder power right hand off of my skull. This one wobbled me, and I staggered into the fence. As I pushed off the fence to reinstate the clinch, Borders reloaded and landed yet another power shot. My poor cranium. Walking through the fire, I reestablished the clinch and Borders finally whiffed on one of his punches. I had nothing left in the tank, but I knew the round was close to over. I knew I was probably winning at this point, and if I could hang on in all likelihood I'd take the victory.

A flashback from my wrestling days came back to me. I had been winning a match and had gotten thrown to my back. I had been nowhere near getting pinned and had been content to ride it out. While contented, the referee had stolen the match from me by calling the phantom pin. I had gone to complain to my coach, and he had no sympathy for me.

"You got lazy out there. Yes, it was a bad call by the ref, but you got lazy."

Back in the cage now, I told myself, *Dig deep, take him down one more time to secure the victory.*

Running on fumes, I shot in for another takedown. I used all my strength to barely surmount Borders equally aware resistance of what this last takedown meant.

As we crash to the mat, I heard for the first time in the

flight, *THWACK. THWACK. THWACK.*

Two pieces of wood were slamming into each other, signifying the final 10 seconds of the round—in this case the final 10 seconds of the fight. Wanting to look lively and stay active, I delivered seven more of the weakest punches imaginable to Borders ribs, while my head rested on his gut—not having the energy to hold it up. *Just keep punching. It's about to all be over.*

Meanwhile, Borders was focusing all of his effort on my left arm, waiting for just the right moment. With two seconds left, he sprung into action, fast as lightning—as if having energy from the very first round, and threw an armbar attempt. This armbar was by far the deepest and best executed of the many attempts. It was the only one that truly threatened breaking my arm. Of course, it came at the end when my guard may have been down and I had nothing left in the tank. I reacted, as quickly as my body would allow, into a hyper-defensive posture. The armbar was so deep that I was not trying to free it, just defend so he didn't break my arm. Barely but successfully defending, the bell rang one final time. *Ding!*

Thirty-four

By The Skin of My Teeth

The ref rushed to stop the fight. I quickly got to my feet and threw my arms over my head, signifying victory. Directly afterward, I collapsed into a squat from sheer exhaustion. I took a few deep breaths and forced myself back to my feet. I didn't want to feed any judges' imagination that I might have lost that fight. Once on my feet again, I raised my arms in victory again and began to walk to the edge of the cage to look out into the crowd full of my supporters for the first time. On my way over, I was

117

intercepted by the cage-side physician.

"Are you feeling OK?"

I glanced at him, shot him a quick, "Yeah," and walked right by him.

Already passed him, he asked, "Any nausea or headache?"

Without even turning to face him, I shook my head no in response. After taking the cheering reception of my supporters, I continued to walk around the cage to catch my breath. Brian and Max entered the cage to go over and congratulate Borders and his coaches on a good fight.

On his way over, Brian congratulated me. "Good job, kid!"

Max gave me a hug, uncaring about the sweaty mess that I was, still covered in some Borders' blood. He then walked over to offer the other corner the same congratulations that Brian just had.

Brian walked back over and put his hand on my back. "Proud of you, kid."

"Thanks man," I answered shortly, still trying to catch my breath.

"I told you a sanctioned MMA fight was going to be a different level."

I shook my head not to disagree, but out of the disbelief of how true of a statement that was. "I had never been hit so hard in my life."

"Told ya!"

Borders made his way over to where Brian and I were chatting. I saw him come over out of the corner of my eye and looked up. I raised my hand to slap him a high-five for a good fight, and Borders nodded and extended his hand in agreement. We slapped five and embraced each other in a hug.

On the break, my eyes got wide, showing sincerity. I pointed to him. "Dude! You hit hard!"

He pointed back to me to return the compliment, but sort of realized that I didn't hit quite as hard. I think what he meant to say was something like, "Man, you're tough."

We were interrupted by his coach coming over to me to shake my hand and offer me congratulations on a good fight, sparing any awkwardness of recognizing my weaker punches. Borders' second coach came over to me, and on his way, I gave him a bow of respect similar to that which is offered in Jiu-Jitsu classes and shook his hand. While I shook Borders' coaches' hand, the realization that Borders himself had hurt me multiple times and came painfully close to winning the fight washed over him. He tilted his head to the side and mouthed a profanity to himself, realizing he probably let this one slip away from him. He placed his hands on his hips in an act of his own disapproval of his performance.

A third coach came over to shake my hand and take his turn of congratulating me on a good fight. The referee reemerged and grabbed my hand by the meaty part where the thumb extends from, and did the same to Borders as the announcer neared reading out the judges' decision.

He knocked Borders' hand and mine into each other as he tells us, "Good fight boys."

I then felt him raise my hand as if in declaring victory, and I responded by raising my other arm in agreement. The crowd erupted in cheers as I snuck a peek to see what Borders was doing. Turns out, the ref had raised his arm as well to signify the good competitive fight we both had shared.

Interesting side note: Borders did not raise his other arm. When the ref lowered our arms, preparing to receive the decision, my other arm lingered in the air a little longer, and I pumped my fist before lowering it, claiming victory for myself.

I was still breathing heavy and rocking back and forth to help take my mind off the pain in my lungs. Those judges sure seemed like they were taking their sweet time, and I was starting to get worried something fishy might be going on. The ref still holding our hands in the center of the cage took it upon himself to break that awkward pause and told Borders and I a joke as he slapped our hands together a couple of more times.

"Alright boys, turns out the judges missed the fight and we're going to have run it back again right now."

I let out a chuckle, and the ref started laughing hysterically, cracking himself up. Borders merely smirked as he realized he did pine for another chance. He was hanging his head and briefly looked up and mouthed that profanity one more time. He then leaned into the ref in hopes that only he could hear.

"Just takedowns," he said with a protesting smile, seeking approval.

The ref shook his head and said matter-of-factly, "You gotta be able to stop the takedown in this sport."

Borders looked away, to his corner, not getting the reassurance he was looking for. His corner told him to raise his arm to signify victory, and Borders began to comply, but after only raising it halfway, he swung it back down, hitting his own thigh as he shook his head in understanding at the inauthenticity behind it. I pretended not to hear any of it. The ref slapped our hands together a few more times.

I was still rocking back and forth and breathing heavily to catch my breath. Still waiting there in the middle of that cage, which seemed like more time than the fight itself, the ref himself was starting to act antsy. He looked back to the judges to see what was going on. He nervously slapped Borders' and my hands together a few more times still.

The music died down, and the announcer came on over the loudspeakers. "OK ladies and gentleman after three rounds we go to the judges' scorecards…"

I held my breath—the one I hadn't even caught back yet. "Judge Velasquez scored the fight 29-28 for the blue corner…" *Shit*. If it was a unanimous decision, the announcer would have said something like, "All three judges scored the contest 29-28 for the winner by

120

unanimous decision, the blue corner, Dave Greenberg," or maybe "Judge Velasquez scored the fight 30-27 and the remaining judges scored the fight 29-28 for the winner by unanimous decision, in the blue corner, Dave Greenberg." But, that's not how it was going to go down. Nonetheless, the crowd cheered as one judge scored it for me, and I acknowledged the crowd by briefly raising up my arm before dropping it disappointedly. It was not going to be a unanimous decision, and I was fearful I may not have won on the majority of the judges' scorecards.

"Judge Leggie scored the fight 29-28 for the red corner…"

The crowd booed as Borders raised his arm and then pounded his chest as he nodded in approval, as if to say, "Good look man, respect."

"And Judge Krawiec scores the fight 29-28, for the winner by split decision…" My heart skipped a beat. *They better not have stolen this from me.*

"From the *blue* corner, for *Daaavvveeee Greeeeeenbeerrrrry!!!*"

I raised my own arms in hard-fought victory as the crowd erupted once more.

Leading up to the fight, I envisioned every possible scenario and even the possibility that this outcome might happen. Sometimes I envisioned winning quickly with a knockout or a submission and sometimes I envisioned winning after a long, grueling beating that I had to take, overcoming it for the victory. In every imagined account I would come out the victor—I made sure of it. Secretly though, I wanted a fight where I was getting my ass kicked, even bloodied up, where I would be able to show my heart and what I was made of. While I didn't get bloodied up, I got injured far worse and came way closer to defeat (multiple times) than I had imagined, even in the worst of the scenarios. Still, I was happy for the opportunity to show what I was made of in front of so many loved ones. Hard-fought as it was, I didn't know it yet, but this would prove to be the easy stuff.

Thirty-five

Heart, Chin, & Lungs

The promoter's concern of my supporters leaving right after my fight was a valid one. Exiting the cage and then the theater, I was met by everyone who had shown up for me right in the foyer. Their cheers were absolutely overwhelming. After their ovation died down, they all spontaneously broke into a chant.

"Meanberg! Meanberg! Meanberg!"

My heart was smiling as wide as the one on my face, and I was only barely able to hold back tears. My 11-year-old brother (probably a little too young to be watching this sort of event) came running over and hugged me tighter than he ever had before. I embraced him and hugged him back equally as tight. The overfilled hallway of my supporters and passersby all let out a collective "Awwwww." Everyone circled around and took their turns hugging me, patting my back and congratulating me on my achievement. The whole experience really was humbling. Thankfully before my emotions could be completely overwhelmed, a few of my friends proudly presented me the gigantic fight card poster they had nicked from the wall. Complete with my newly minted record, they crossed out the first "0" of my 0-0 record and overlaid it with a "1." They were pretty proud of themselves, and I was a little embarrassed but also immensely grateful.

I eventually was able to excuse myself so I could go back to the staging area to put on some more clothes and collect my things. It was back in that area when Brian imparted some more wisdom on me.

"You know why you won the fight right?"

"Because I stopped overthinking? Because I was able to finally get the fight to the ground?"

"Sure, but more than those things—it's because you

have a chin and can take a nasty shot that might put down a horse. Because you had the lungs to push the pace on Borders. And because you've got heart kid—you never gave up."

"Thanks man."

"When we get back to the gym we'll work on a better defense—perhaps better head movement so you don't have to rely so heavily on that granite chin of yours. Meanwhile, enjoy the rest of the weekend here in AC. Wish I could spend it with you and your wild and crazy fans, but my wife would kill me if I left her with the rug rats. Proud of you kid."

"Ha, thanks man, and thanks for everything you did to help me win this thing."

I took a moment to reflect before rejoining my group of friends and family. It had taken everything I had to barely win an amateur MMA fight by split decision against an 0-1 opponent. I revealed my ability to overcome adversity by battling through a herniated disc, being dropped unconscious (that later proved to be a concussion), and coming to the physical and spiritual brink brought about by one hellish choke. I was grateful that I had not only gotten the victory but had also fulfilled my hope of showing what I was made of. I will say though, "Careful what you wish for." It may just be more than you bargained for. My doubters fueled me. My supporters buoyed me. And I invested in myself. I never worked so hard for something in my life. That hard work was the "lungs" part of the equation. Again, I barely won. Imagine I did one less hill sprint, or was slightly less strict on my diet—almost anything could have tipped the scales in the other direction when the margin of victory was so thin. I was merely gifted with my chin, but my heart was strengthened by the hard work I put in as well as by the people pulling for me.

On behalf of my heart, I want to take a second to thank each and every one of my supporters who believed in me even when my own seeds of doubt were creeping in. To all my doubters—told you so. Let that be a lesson to you, I wouldn't bet against me.

In addition to all of the supporters that made it out, there were a number of my closest friends that couldn't attend my fight. Between those two groups, two stood out—with the shared name Nick [neither Pickles (I guess I have a lot of friends named Nick)]. Both were to attend another friend's wedding in the southeast. The first Nick drove from to New York to my fight, and without even being able to stick around to congratulate me or come out with us, he hit the road to drive through the night to make the wedding. He is one of the hardest working people I know and is an eternal source of inspiration for me. I am supremely grateful for his sacrifice to show his support. The second Nick was the same one who showed up to my BJJ tournament and took me out, boasting about me. Nick was already down for the wedding but refused to miss the fight. Despite having to take care of wedding obligations, he snuck away to watch the fight on his laptop as it streamed. He was in a local bar, going crazy throughout the ups and downs of the fight. He was asked numerous times to simmer down to which he responded,

"There's no way I will calm down. That's my buddy!"

Nick's personality had it such that before long, the whole bar was huddled around his laptop cheering me on from hundreds of miles away. In his elation at my victory, he celebrated hard. Perhaps a little too hard. One of the duties assigned to him was to look after all of the shoes for the wedding party after they were used to determine height order for photos the day before the wedding. Nick lost all of the shoes and was forced to scramble the morning of the wedding to go out and buy all of the wedding party new shoes. A truer friend there is not.

Returning to my friends and family back at Atlantic City, we all walked back to the hotel we were staying at. Not everyone was able to stay for the weekend, and for those that had to leave, I hugged and thanked them again for all of their support. There were about 50 of us that remained. We all washed up and changed into clothes more suitable for nightlife and hit the town. I have to say when you're rolling as deep as we were, after our shared victory in a place like Atlantic City, it made for quite the experience. Tired, but content—I felt completely blessed as the night wore on and I got too drunk.

One of the very best weekends of my life eventually was over. All good things must come to an end. I said my thanks and goodbyes to those that remained for the duration of the weekend. Instinctually I waited until everyone had left before I packed up myself. Gear gathered and loaded like that pack mule, I pushed the button for the elevator. As I waited for the elevator to arrive atop the tower I was staying in on that busy overcrowded end of the weekend when everyone in the hotel was seemingly checking out all at once, I walked over to the window overlooking the beach and the Atlantic Ocean. It really wasn't until that moment when I was alone with my thoughts and nowhere pressing to be did it all sink in. I had been granted the enormous blessing of realizing a dream. Interestingly, there is a surreal feeling associated with realizing a dream—almost indistinguishable from when your dreaming. *Did that really happen? Did I really do that?* As the rhythmic, hypnotic waves crashed onto the beach, I felt a sort of peace and confirmation I was right where I belonged.

Ding. Not the fight bell, but the elevator's arrival snapped me back to reality. If we're lucky, we have transcendent, pinnacle moments in our life. If luckier still, we can recognize them when they're happening. I hope it doesn't come off as greedy or ungrateful, but I hope to return to that state from time to time. One thing I do know—it'll take everything I have for just the chance to attain it ever again, but I'm willing to invest just for the chance.

Thirty-six

Unintended Consequences

One challenge leading up to the fight I haven't commented on yet was my love interest at the time. We only went on a handful of dates in the weeks leading up to the fight, but we went hiking through the woods and talked about philosophy and life, and if that wasn't enough, the way she wore flowers in her hair really started in on my heart. I felt myself getting distracted from the fight and realized how that could be a fatal flaw. I asked her if it was OK that we took a small break from dating so I could focus the crescendo of my fight training, and she kindly agreed.

It was the day before I would be leaving to travel down to Atlantic City for the fight, and she hadn't wished me luck or reached out to me. While poking around the Facebook event my buddy Chris had organized for the weekend, she popped up, having just changed her default photo. It was her with her ex-boyfriend, making out.

What the hell?! She couldn't tell me, or at least wait until after my fight to post that picture with this dude's tongue down her throat?

Needless to say, that filled me with a certain rage that I did my best to channel.

This is pertinent because while I might have liked to "celebrate" with her after my triumph, I was all by my lonesome. Now please bear with me as I attempt to broach the highly uncomfortable topic of self-love. There is a reason for it—I promise.

My first conceptualization of what it meant to masturbate was an overly naïve one. I knew that I liked looking at scantily clothed woman from an early age—I mean a very early age. Before I knew about sex or masturbation, I knew I liked women, but I didn't exactly understand why. One Sunday afternoon, my parents took my sister and me to the boardwalk for a day of family fun.

I was about four years old. Upon exiting the car, I saw a woman in her early twenties. She had straight long blonde hair, blue eyes, and tan skin. She was wearing a jean skirt with a white blouse and red high heels. She offered me an easy smile before catching up with the group she was with. This obviously left quite the impression on me as I can still remember it vividly thirty years later. Still relatively new to the world, and curious, I decided to ask my dad about it.

"Dad?"

"Yes Dave?"

"How come when I see a pretty girl my penis gets hard?"

As smart of a man my dad is, I don't think he could have guessed that question coming in a million years, especially from his four-year-old son. He laughed nervously, but hardily and stumbled through his best attempt explaining how it was normal and natural, going into as little detail as possible. Afterward, I don't know for a fact that my dad thought to himself, *That's my boy,* but I just know it's true.

Fast forward about one decade and puberty, with its hormonal assault, took something that was merely curious just a few years earlier and turned it into the subject of preoccupation. Very attracted to women by my early teens and having seen a few raunchy films like *There's Something About Mary* with various masturbation scenes—I knew there was a desirable outcome there. I vaguely knew the mechanics but believed that one had to achieve the perfect mental state of beauty and love to coincide with the mechanics to achieve climax. As such, the act almost became more of meditation practice, trying to reach transcendence all the while playing with my dick. Needless to say, I was unsuccessful—at achieving climax or transcendence.

It wasn't until after football practice on the late bus home that perhaps the dumbest troublemaker in the whole school was talking about how great it was to jerk off. How could it be this dumb, unsophisticated joker could have figured this out before me? There was no way he had the mental capacity to reach that serene meditative mental state required to achieve the beauty of an orgasm. Right?! Well on the off chance this schlub knew something I didn't, I thought that maybe I should listen to what he had to say.

"You look at the dirty picture to get your dick hard, and then your hand takes over and that's it."

He can't be right, how can such a profound experience be so overly simple, I thought to myself.

Later that night without any better strategy than the dumb tutorial Jimmy Purrizella offered, I figured, what could it hurt to try it out? Holy shit—dumb Jimmy Purrizella was right! Let's do that again! Oh, ok, ok, that's now how that works, I painfully learned. I had just discovered my new favorite pastime.

After a while of looking at the same Sears magazine lingerie section, one wants for more. It just so happened that my parents had just upgraded our television cable package, and whilst flipping through the channels, I came across some adult content. I was sure to keep flipping as I wasn't home alone, but made a very pronounced mental note of this new advent and stored it for when I would be home alone next.

It wasn't before long when that scenario happened. I woke up quite excited. I knew where everyone was going to be for the day, and I had hours of freedom. I cracked open my bedroom door and called out "Hello? Anybody home?" Silence. How golden. I proceed to strut downstairs naked and began to set up my masturbation station.

Paper towels laid out, hand lotion acquired, and now all I had to do was flip on that glorious adult content. Keep in mind this was in a time when internet porn constituted waiting five minutes for a single photo to download. Access to video was a game changer. The television was turned on, and all I had to do was click to that magical channel. *This Channel is Parentally Blocked. Please enter passcode.* Dammit! This could not be happening right now.

Now some people would admit defeat and bust out their Sears catalog and get on with their day. Not this stubborn teen. Like a dog and his bone—I had a focus. I rummaged through the end tables, desperately looking for the cable box manual. Found it. Now to the parental password section. OK, 5-10 procedures to follow and each successful step taken felt like passing a level in a video game—with way more at stake and the best reward I might ever attain awaiting completion. All the steps followed except for one final one: enter the passcode you previously selected. *Now what would my dad enter, hmm?*

After a couple of failed attempts, a warning flashed on the screen. *Last attempt or screen gets locked for 24 hours.* Now this is where a reasonable person would cut their losses, but not your boy. *Think Dave, think Dave. Dad might realize he might forget the very code he inputted. How might that influence the code he chooses? I bet he put in the example code from the manual figuring he might forget himself. He'll reference the manual and bam there it'll be.* A good theory, right? Not just a good theory, my early teen self figured that shit out. *Boom, I'm in.*

There were three channels with the adult content that I was flipping between. Just as I was getting into it, I thought I heard something outside the front of the house. I paused for a moment to listen more intently. I didn't hear anything and convinced myself I was just being overly paranoid. *You know where everyone is for the day. Relax and enjoy this.* I got back to business, but then that little voice went off in my head again. *Ya know, I'll be able to enjoy this more if I just go and make sure it really isn't anything.* I walk over to the front door and look through the window. To my sheer horror, I saw my dad's car pulling into the garage. "Holy Shit!" I ran upstairs as fast as I could and retreated to my room. As I began to catch my breath, it dawned on me: the tv was still on with the porn blasting, and my masturbation station was still on display front and center. Without having time to put on any clothes, I raced back downstairs into the family room. I promptly changed the channel and turned off the tv. I could now see my dad at the front door (our garage did not have an entrance into the house) from the family room through the hallway. I still had to deal with all of my paraphernalia. It was bulky and awkward, and I feared if I tried to run upstairs with it, I'd drop the bottle of lotion or whatever else. I hurriedly scooped everything in one fell swoop and buried it into the couch cushions. My dad was still at the front door, not expecting the door to be locked (thank God, in my preparation that was one step I didn't neglect). As I was now dashing to get back upstairs, I had to pass directly through my dad's line of sight. As I hit the hallway, which the front door opened into, I could see the lock turning to the unlocked position. Unable to bolt up the stairs because the angle would betray my position and my dad would have a clear look at my bare ass hightailing it up the stairs, I made the bold and unexpected decision to sprint in the direction of the front door. The window on the front door was only on the top half of the door. So, from about ten feet away already in a full naked sprint, I hit the deck and slid right to the bottom opaque part of the door with my dad still fumbling right above me now. "Shit, shit, shit! What am I going to do?!" I looked up and immediately to my left was our downstairs bathroom. As slyly as I could, I maneuvered myself into the bathroom—half army crawling, half back against the wall. Just as I made it into the bathroom, I closed the door simultaneously as my dad opened the front door.

"Hey Dave! I'm home early. I had a couple of patient cancelations!" my dad called out, thinking I was upstairs.

"Oh, hey Dad. I'm in the bathroom."

"Oh ok."

My dad then went into the kitchen to fix himself lunch. My dad was a creature of habit and would sit in "his" chair at the kitchen table any time he was in the kitchen. The kitchen was off of the hallway but had an obscured view to most of the hallway from how it was situated. Now you might be thinking—I was in the clear. I could just exit the bathroom wrapped in a towel and complete my grand escape. You'd be wrong though—sorely wrong. The downstairs bathroom was only a half-bath. That is to say, there was no shower. Moreover, with no shower that meant no full-sized towels. There I was staring at the two hand towels hanging from rings on the wall thinking, *What good are those things going to do me?* Furthermore, because there was no shower on the first floor, there was absolutely no reason for me to be naked down here (save for masturbating), and that's something I'd just soon as avoid having to share with my dad.

Knowing the layout of the first floor and where my dad would be sitting, there was just a narrow sliver of the hallway my dad would be able to see. Of course, that narrow sliver covered the first five stairs to our split-level house. Once past those five stairs though, it was clear sailing out of view all the way up the rest of my stairs and to my room. I devised a plan that I needed to cover that distance of the viewable portion of the hallway from my dad's purchase in the kitchen as fast and silently as possible. What better way to do that than by jumping those five stairs all at once. Sure, my landing would make a ruckus, but I'd already be out of sight by then. Now I understood this was a high risk, high reward gambit. Should I not make it, I'd crash loudly, probably injured, with my dad coming over to stand over me while I rolled around the floor naked in pain. Best I put that thought out of my mind. I counted to three and went for it. I began my silent sprint and as I approached my launch point, putting everything I had into it. It was at this moment, time slowed down for me. I was soaring through the air naked in slow-motion, and it dawned on me, *I'm gonna make it!*

Now, I don't know what possessed me, but I figured

seeing what my dad was up to might be useful. Still in slow motion, I begin to turn my head to look through the doorway of the kitchen to make sure I had gotten away with it. As my head finished turning, allowing me to peer into the kitchen, I was greeted with the worst thing imaginable—my dad just happened to be looking through the doorway at the very moment. Still locked in slow motion, and still flying through the air naked, my dad and I made perfect, unbroken, unwavering eye contact, tracking the entire duration of my slow-motion flight, which felt like 15 seconds in real time. I traversed the stairs, hit the ground with a thud, and time sped right back up. "WHY GOD?! WHY?!" I cringed so hard I thought I might have pulled a muscle. I shook it off, ran upstairs, put some clothes on, ran back downstairs, and said, "Hey Dad, how was work?" Without listening to the answer, I went into the family room, collected the remnants of my masturbation station, hid them under my sweatshirt, went back to my room, and died of embarrassment. My dad and I to this day have not discussed our moment in time locked in one another's gaze as I flew through air naked.

Well over a decade later, I would have to eventually pay the piper and discuss with my dad a masturbation experience. A few days after the fight, without the girl I was seeing right before I had left due to her suddenly important timing to get back with her ex, I was left on my own to take care of any sexual frustration I was suffering. Thankfully I had mastered the art of stealth and privacy by then. My problem this time was of a whole new, much more serious variety. In the middle of the act, doing the deed, as I got closer and closer to climax, that pleasurable sensation linked up to a pain in my head. The nearer I got to climax, the worse the corresponding pain in my head would get. It got so bad that I stopped. For two reasons really—the first being that the pain got so intense that it just wasn't worth the pleasurable sensation. Second and much more frightening, I was worried that by attaining an orgasm, something might burst inside my head.

OK that was weird.

I decided to pretend like it didn't happen. A few more days went by, and I worked up the nerve to try again. Lo and behold, the exact same thing happened. I was legitimately freaked out at this point, and I decided to do the worst thing possible—look on the internet for what it might be. I found a few entries on various medical websites for "sex headaches." Turns out, they're a real thing, not something one of my girlfriends was making up when she wasn't in the mood. Jokes aside, this is what I read:

"Sex headaches are brought on by sexual activity — especially an orgasm. You may notice a dull ache in your head and neck that builds up as sexual excitement increases. Or, more commonly, you may experience a sudden, severe headache just before or during orgasm. May be a symptom of an aneurism caused by a blow to the head."

I forewent all embarrassment and called my dad up and read to him what I had just read. Now my dad has a doctor's sense of humor and would often make the laid up softball joke. When I'd tell him it hurt when I did this or that he'd respond, "Don't do this or that. That'll be fifty dollars." Even when he wasn't joking, he'd be way calmer in any sort of emergency or various symptom freak and answer something to the effect of, "Relax, you're full of it and worrying yourself for no reason."

But when I got done reading him the passage, this time, however, he answered, "Huh?"

"HUH?! HUH?! WHAT DO YOU MEAN HUH?!"

"Relax, it's probably nothing. I just want to confer with one of my specialist colleagues to confirm."

That next day, waiting for my dad to get back to me was a long one. People could die of aneurisms. Even if it wasn't that, I was imagining never being able to enjoy sex again. I was a wreck. My dad finally called me back.

"Listen Dr. So-and-so, thinks it's probably nothing to be concerned about. At least not at this stage. He said it's likely a combination of you eating super clean and restricting alcohol for the months leading up to your fight, followed by a drunken weekend after your fight. You didn't get the much sleep before your fight because of the nerves, and you didn't get enough after the fight because of going out. All that in conjunction with the concussion you likely suffered from being momentarily knocked unconscious in the fight is likely all it is. Stay away from alcohol for a little while, make sure you get enough sleep, and everything should return to normal on its own."

"Are you sure? What if it doesn't?"

In his calm voice, he reassured me. "If it's still a problem, we'll cross that bridge when we come to it and order any tests we need to, but it's probably nothing. That'll be fifty bucks."

"Ha-ha, very funny Dad."

Thank goodness he was right (as he usually is).

Thirty-seven

Back to Reality

After the fight, I was riding a pretty substantial high for a little while. I attended barbeques, traveled a bit, and then got back into the nitty-gritty of graduate school. As I entered my last year, it was differentiated from the previous year by my guidance counseling internship in a New Jersey public high school. I showed up for the new staff orientation, and I did just that—became oriented with this new system. The orientation spanned a few days, and on the last day, just before the kids came back to school from summer break, my new boss called the first meeting of the year with the entire counseling staff. After the staff went around sharing what they had done for summer, my turn in the rotation came up. Getting ready to try on my best humble-brag for winning a cage fight in Atlantic City as my noteworthy activity for the summer, something a bit out of the ordinary I thought, especially for a counselor, my boss, John, chimed in before I could say anything.

"Hi all, I hope you had a good summer. As some of you know, we are lucky enough to have the extra support of an intern this year. I will be splitting his time between all six of you over the course of the year. I have had the chance to meet with David over the last few days, and I can tell you all that he is a fine young man. Now he's pretty shy and wouldn't bring it up on his own…"

I thought, *Man he doesn't know me well enough yet*, in my relatively young and eager state. *I am all too ready to share my conspicuous news having won a fight.*

"He earned a Good Samaritan Award a little while back. OK David, why don't you tell us all that story?"

I was totally blindsided. Like I said I was all too happy to boast, but even I had limits. I took a second to collect my thoughts and began in on that story.

Part III

Transforming Luck

Thirty-eight

Fumbling Forward

My supervisor for my practicum (the precursor to my internship) placement also happened to be a doctorate level counselor, professor, and critically a professional resume writer, which happened to be particularly useful when my sister and I had a difference of opinion on what ought and ought not be included on a resume.

"Dave, how do you include the Good Samaritan Award on your resume? I'm writing mine now and don't know how to include it?" Cindy asked.

Astonishingly my sister and I were both awarded a Good Samaritan Award for our efforts in the same event. "What? Why would you include that on your resume? It has nothing to do with the work either of us do."

"Umm I'm pretty sure that is something we should include on our resumes," she said, with the disbelief I hadn't known this.

"Umm I'm pretty sure you're wrong," I responded in a mocking tone that only an older brother could summon when talking to a younger sibling.

"Listen, my site supervisor is a professional resume writer in addition to her other competencies. Let me run it by her and I'll get back to you."

"OK thanks let me know."

I cautiously knocked on my supervisor's door with a light enough touch that perhaps she might not have heard. For I was embarrassed to bring up such a topic with her. "Come in," my supervisor permitted. I walked in slowly with a slight unease. I might have been a little too deferential, but it was a practice of mine that if I was going to err, I'd much prefer it be in that direction.

A little background before the content of this meeting: I was the only student in my cohort that elected to do their practicum at the university level. The format was a practicum one semester that preceded a two-semester long internship. The practicum and internship could not be with the same age grouping for the students. We could choose elementary school, middle school, high school, or college. In my university practicum placement, I had earned the esteem and confidence of my supervisor to be able to meet with students one-on-one to help them with a host of academic topics. I found this to be extremely rewarding.

After establishing a good rapport with one of my students in particular, she felt comfortable enough to share with me that she was having suicidal thoughts. Knowing right away that I was in over my head, but that this student trusted me enough with something as deeply personal and painful, I honored and respected it at as such. I made sure to reassure and support the student. I relayed that her ability to share these deeply painful thoughts was indication of strength and was admirable, despite those thoughts trying to communicate to her that she was weak. Being present, attentive, and authentically caring took paramount importance. I was thankful that the training and support of my professors and supervisors allowed for a circumstance to help a student that was really hurting. Not only did it work out for this student (thank goodness), but it shined a positive light on me in my supervisor's eyes. As such I was receiving a lot of admiration from my boss and professors—I wasn't totally comfortable with it because I was still so new to my training. So, the idea of having to bring up a Good Samaritan Award to my supervisor felt a little too self-congratulatory, but for my sister, I went ahead anyway.

"Come in," Dr. Georges beckoned.

"Hi Dr. Georges, if now isn't a good time I can come back," I suggestively hoped.

"No no, don't be silly. Of course I have time for my standout student," she half-ribbed, half-venerated. I blushed. "Come on in, take a seat." I obliged. "What can I do for you David?"

"I have sort of an odd question related to your other discipline of resume writing."

"Sure of course, happy to help."

"OK well my sister is writing her resume and she reached out to me asking how to include one thing in particular on her resume, and I didn't think it belonged because it was unrelated to our disciplines. We both earned a Good Samaritan Award."

"Oh, my that's very impressive. What did you do to earn a Good Samaritan Award?"

"I was sort of hoping to spare you all that."

"David, you aren't sparing me if I ask. Not to mention, the context will help me answer if it belongs on your and your sister's resume."

"I suppose you're right. Alright, here it goes…"

Thirty-nine

Is This Real Life?

My parents, sister, and I were out to dinner at a waterfront restaurant on the north shore of Long Island. It was late August, and after dinner we all decided to go for a walk on the boardwalk under the stars, overlooking where the Nissequogue River empties into the Long Island Sound. Less than five minutes into our stroll the most unbelievable thing happened. It was the first and only time in my life where I didn't believe my eyes in real time.

Out of nowhere, a car came barreling past the security booth, careening through the parking lot at about 40 mph down the boat ramp, crashing into the water. The cognitive dissonance that washed over me could best be explained like a dream state. In fact, due to the irregularity and peculiarity, I actually thought I was dreaming. Just then my sister let out a blood-curdling scream, which snapped me back into reality—strange as it was. Without so much as a thought, instinct took over.

I took off in a full sprint after the car that was drifting further and further from the shore. My instinctual "plan" was to run to the boat ramp about a hundred yards away, run down said boat ramp, and jump up on to a pier that extended beyond the boat ramp about another hundred feet, which was where the car had drifted out to by the time I started my pursuit. Best laid plans of mice and men...once I hit the boat ramp at full clip, it took all of my agility to not face-plant due to the ramp being covered in some sort of extremely treacherous algae. I could hear my sister trailing behind me and fearing for her safety, I frantically called back to her.

"SLOW DOWN! SLOW DOWN SLOW DOWN! THE RAMP IS CRAZY SLIPPERY!!!"

Unable to make the leap from the boat ramp to the pier because of my compromised footing, I dove into the water from the boat ramp itself. Unfortunately for my sister, she received my announcement just as she had taken her first step on to the dangerously slippery boat ramp and hit the brakes at that inopportune time. I didn't find out until after the ordeal, but as a result of pulling the brakes on a slippery surface, my poor sister wasn't able to avoid the inevitable face-plant, and with the speed she was carrying, entered the water with the grace of a seal sliding on her belly.

I've always been a pretty strong swimmer, and in college I took a physical education course in lifeguarding. I even elected to get the extra waterfront certification (thank goodness for that). One major difference from all of my training though: I was never in a rescue situation where I had to swim with all of my clothes on—oh well, never had to deal with any sort of automobile waterfront rescue either.

I was swimming as fast as I could to get to the car, not knowing when it might sink. Thankfully the car was simply and oddly just floating at the surface. Swimming with the extra resistance of all my clothes not only severely slowed my pace but also required loads more effort, and that was just to get to the car. Just as I was nearing the still drifting car, a gentleman from the restaurant had a direct line to the pier, allowing him to avoid the perilous boat ramp and took the route I had hoped to take. He ran the length of the pier and dove in right next to me just a few feet from the car now. Meanwhile, my sister was overcome by the drag of her clothing against the resisting water. She elected to lighten her load before carrying on. She swam over to the pier to take off her sneakers and placed them on to the pier. With all the commotion, a crowd began to form, and they approached my sister as she was placing her shoes on the pier.

"Is the water deep?"

"Yeah, if you can't swim don't come in."

"Is the water cold?"

"What?! Yes, I'm a little busy to be talking about the temperature of the water," jeered Cindy.

Sneakers jettisoned, distractors derided, and she was back on her way with the rescue effort. Cindy swam up to the floating car where the gentleman from the restaurant and I were evaluating the situation. Merely approaching the decade-old compact car, the overpowering odor of alcohol emanated from the open window. Surveying the circumstance, we noticed it was just the driver in the car.

"Hey man, are you ok?"

The driver slowly turned his head from facing forward to look at us. He was so drunk that he couldn't answer us.

"OK, we're going to get you out of here."

Since the driver was not wearing his seatbelt, I tried to lift him up and out through the open window. Trouble was, without the ground to stand on for leverage, instead of the driver being lifted up, I descended upon applying the force. Quickly realizing I was not going to be able to lift him, I reached into the window to unlock the door from the inside.

"We're going to have to open the door to get him out!" I announced. The gentleman and I positioned ourselves to grip the door while placing our feet at fixed places on the automobile. There had not been a countdown; we just were psychically in sync. We both applied our full strength to open the door. Despite the back pressure of the water, the door opened relatively easy—no doubt thanks to our pumping adrenal glands.

As soon as we got the door open, the water started to rush in, and the car began to sink. The rate at which it was sinking made it so that in five seconds the entire car was submerged. Now, that sounds a lot faster than it actually was, especially that all it would take for the driver to exit the vehicle at this point was to lean to his left. That's it, just lean to his left.

One, one thousand. "Get out of the car."

Two, one thousand. "Get out of the car!"

Three, one thousand. "Get out of the car!"

Four, one thousand. *"GET THE FUCK OUT OF THE CAR!!!"*

Five, one thousand—with the driver's pale blue eyes looking dead into mine, he cut into my soul and disappeared into the murky abyss. My very first thought was, *No. I will not have the memory of a man dying right in front me*, and with that, I took a quick breath.

As soon I was submerged, I found myself completely blind from the dark waters and dove sightless after the sinking car. I prayed as I dove, *Please God, let me find the car.* Losing orientation in the blackness, I kept pursuing after the sinking car. After 15 seconds, I had still not located the car. At this time the thought of surfacing for a fuller breath entered my consciousness. After quickly contemplating that approach, I dismissed it and put it out of my head, understanding that I had zero chance of locating the car if

I surfaced and dove back down—so deeper I went. Finally, after about 10 more seconds, my probing hand contacted the car. *Alright!* Still blind, I presumed what I was touching was the roof of the car. Assuming I was right, I used that contact point to construct a mental model of the car.

If this is the roof, then the opening to the door should be here....

I swung my arm through the emptiness. *Nothing!* I kept sweeping back and forth and still couldn't locate the guy. Just when I thought all hope was lost and that the driver may have been expelled from the vehicle and could be anywhere, I thought I felt the faintest thing brush up against the back of my hand. I grabbed for what I thought I felt, but wasn't convinced. I pulled a second a time, and I felt a little resistance. It wound up being his shirt (now a T-shirt in water doesn't feel like much in part due to its elasticity). I had him though! I sured up my grip and began to surface with him. I only was able to take a couple of surfacing strokes before we got snagged. He was getting snagged on the car itself. You see, when the car door had been opened and the water had rushed in, the weight of the water had pushed the part of the car where the water had been entering downward. The car door opening was now facing the river bottom. Still without the use of sight, as the car, the driver, and myself were still sinking (I was told later it ended up being 50 feet deep), I was able to conceptualize what must have happened to the orientation of the car. Upon that realization, I swam down below the car, pulled the man down and out to clear the opening, and then began to surface with him.

I broke the surface and took a breath of air like it was the first breath I had ever taken. Out of the corner my eye, I saw my sister preparing to dive, and I started shouting,

"I've got him! I've got him! I've got him!"

Later my sister told me she was thinking, *If you've got him...he needs to breathe too...you should bring him to the surface also.*

What she wasn't taking into account was not only did I

have to swim a 200+ lb. man up from the depths, but I was working against the drag of all of my clothes and all of his clothes. It took an extra second to pull him all the way up to the surface. While all of that craziness was happening, my parents were on the sidelines, readying themselves to perform CPR or whatever else the circumstance called for. Turns out from their perspective, the way the car sank and how quickly I dove after it made it seem to them that I was trapped by the sinking car and dragged under. So, when I surfaced, they were overcome with relief. In a similar vein, Cindy told me afterward that when she was taking a breath to dive, it wasn't for the automobilist. She was preparing to dive after me because she thought I was down there for too long—she estimated over two minutes.

By the time I was able to get the driver to the surface, there were already multiple police cars and ambulances on the scene. I remember marveling just how quickly they were able to arrive. *How long had I been down there?* I thought. Turns out, there had been reports of a drunk driver in the area and as such, police were patrolling the nearby area. When they got the call, they were able to report in scant time. As the three of us were swimming the motorist to shore, our guy spoke for the first time. Upon seeing all of the flashing lights he let out, "Uh-oh."

"Yeah, I know this isn't exactly ideal, but we're still not quite safe yet. Let's keep our focus on getting to shore." I tried my best to console him.

Once we got to where the boat ramp and pier met, I handed him off to the police waiting for us. My sister and I climbed out of the water ourselves and were directed to the ambulances waiting in the parking lot. On the way to the ambulances, my sister collapsed into my arms, and we embraced each other in a hug and began to cry. We told one another we loved each other, and our parents joined our hug and told us, "We're so proud of you. We love you very much."

My sister was treated for minor abrasions from her graceful seal-like entry into the water, and the paramedics took our vitals. My blood pressure was through the roof, and it had the paramedics really concerned. My dad reassured them it was a normal response after the feats I had performed. Once my sister was bandaged up and my blood pressure started to return to normal, we were summoned by the police officers to give statements for what had happened.

Still in our wet clothes and feeling the unseasonable chill in the August nighttime air, we were only provided sheets to be wrapped up in as we waited to give our statements. There were two officers taking statements. My sister and the other gentleman went first. My sister was recounting everything that happened, and when she got to one part in particular, the officer stopped her to presumably teach her something.

"The car sank with the driver still in the car, and my brother dove after the car," Cindy reported.

"Wait," the officer interrupted. "Your brother dove after the submerged vehicle?"

"Yes," my sister responded, thinking to herself, *Didn't I just say that?*

"You know that's really dangerous right?" the officer attempted to educate.

"Uh, yeah…but umm…he had to?" my sister answered in disbelief.

Her tone gave away her perceived absurdity to his statement.

"Well you should know that," he tried to recover.

Cindy estimated that the officer was jealous in a strange way that he didn't have the opportunity to do it himself. The same officer that interviewed my sister interviewed me next. I gave my account of what had happened, and he congratulated me on my "heroic" acts. After all of the accounts were given, all of the first responders circled around us and thanked us for our selfless efforts. Lastly, they finished with a joke that over the years the story would grow and grow, suggesting we'd eventually recount everything that had happened with a school of frenzied sharks circling the whole time. I mean wasn't everything that happened incredible enough? And, besides the water was pitch black; there *could* have been that school of sharks circling us.

It all didn't hit me until we got home and my dad relayed what he had overheard the third Good Samaritan report to the officer.

"Thank God that other guy was there, because there is *no* way I would have been able to do what he did."

My initial instinct was to reject this. "Sure, he would have. He would have had to. He's just saying that."

My sister chimed in. "Dave, I would have tried to do what you did, but I wouldn't have been able to hold my breath that long, let alone be strong enough to swim the driver to the surface."

I grew quiet and introspective in response. The whole thing felt so surreal, like I had just seen a scene from an action movie or something. For the next month or so, I couldn't go more than an hour or so before replaying the whole sequence of events over in my head. It wasn't until weeks later when our dear family friend, the director of our town's chamber of commerce, put us in touch with a reporter for a local publication that we found out that the driver was actually trying to take his own life that night.

Cindy offered up the best outlook in light of that grim news. "Well perhaps now he will make the most of his second chance at life, knowing that even complete strangers care enough to put themselves in harm's way for a stranger."

When I told my friends what had occurred, they initially were in disbelief much like me (and I was there). Soon after though, they busted my balls like only true friends could.

"Dave, so let me get this straight. This guy's life is so

bad, he tries to end it and you not only deny him that, but his car is now at the bottom of Long Island Sound, and he has a DWI to boot to go along with the rest of his troubles. Good job!"

Forty

Confirmation of How Often I'm Wrong

"David, you and your sister absolutely should include that on your resumes!"

"Are you sure? It doesn't come across as boastful or something?"

"David, picture it like this—an employer is conducting a round of interviews to fill a position, and one of the things they're trying to evaluate is if you are the type of person that will stay after hours to get a job done."

"OK?"

"Well, if you're willing to risk your life to save a stranger, might you be the type of person that would stay late and not complain about it?"

"Yes, OK. I see your point."

"Without a shadow of a doubt, you and your sister should include it on your resumes. Let me just say how impressive of a young man I am learning you to be."

"Dr. Georges, I was trying my best not to fish for compliments!" I blushed.

"I know David. It's just been a pleasure to supervise you is all."

My sister was happy to rub it in my face that she was right and I was wrong. I guess I should even be happy about that fact, seeing how it is what set me apart when my boss asked for a stack of resumes from his alma mater (where I luckily happened to attend). Back in that initial meeting when my new boss put me on the spot meeting the rest of the counseling staff, I gave an abridged version of the events to take the spotlight off me as quickly as I could. My boss chimed in after I finished, "When I first saw that on this kid's resume, I thought, *Bullshit!* So, I did a little digging, and when I found out it was true, I just had to have him. Welcome aboard David."

As my hands-on experience grew in my new setting, what grew equally as quickly was my realization that school counseling was not for me. It didn't take long for me to understand that as school counseling was practiced in the "real world," it got bogged down in tons of bureaucratic red tape and even more paperwork. This isn't to deny that all jobs have parts that are unsavory from time to time. It was just that these downsides mapped up to my weaknesses. Take paperwork or more specifically filing for instance: one of my shortcomings of disorganization (something I actively work on still) didn't jive so well together. Worse, I wasn't particularly inspired to get better at this skill—my nature had it that I was much more interested in existential psychotherapy and learning about it. No big deal, surely there were better fitting jobs that perhaps didn't totally do away with the need to be organized, but at least that wouldn't be the lion's share of the work in a given position. Trouble was, all of this was a bit disconcerting, seeing as how I had one year down and one year to go to complete graduate school.

Forty-one

Heartbroken and Confused

In a bit of an existential crisis knowing school counseling wasn't for me and yet stuck on the track of finishing that degree, I reached out to my best buddy John to talk it out and simultaneously take my mind off it. Good friendships handle paradoxes like that no problem. More than that, though, I needed John's comfort more than ever.

My buddy Nick (the Army Ranger who lost everyone's shoes at the wedding because he was too busy cheering me on from afar), had passed away one month earlier. He had been struggling with PTSD from serving overseas and had been dealing with unimaginable things us mere mortals wouldn't have been able to do a fraction as well as he was managing. He had found the strength to fight the stigma of seeking help for what he was battling. This stigma was even stronger in the culture of heroes that Nick belonged to.

Drunk one night and haunted by his memories, he had gone to take his newly prescribed medicine that was supposed to help with the PTSD. That medicine mixed with the alcohol is what had taken him from us friends way too soon. I miss him sorely.

After spending Saturday night taking my mind off the heartbreak of losing a friend, in part by going over my career predicament with John and drowning my sorrows in fast food, we elected to burn off some of those empty calories the next day by going on a hike. Hikes tended to be a good balance of introspective thought, physical exertion, and opportunities to bounce ideas off a trusted friend, plus sweet views. Just what I needed. John had recently bought and moved into his new house with his fiancée at the time. Melissa had graduate school obligations, freeing John for the hike with me. Being new to the area, we googled good hikes in the greater area—landing on Bear Mountain—about a two-hour drive away.

Forty-two

Protective Cloak

As John was approaching my car, he noticed the taped-up rear taillight.

"Dude, what happened to your car?"

"I thought I told you?"

"Nope."

"My cousin's wife, Ellen, accidentally backed into it."

"Shoot, are you going to get it fixed?"

"It's complicated."

"How do you mean?"

"When Ellen came to tell me she accidentally backed into the car, she insisted on paying for the repair. I told her not to worry about it. She was already doing me the huge favor of allowing me to stay with them as I was in grad school. She insisted though. So, I took the car to get an estimate and it wasn't cheap. I knew it wouldn't be."

"How much?"

"Twelve hundred."

"Oof!"

"Yeah."

"So, what are you going to do?"

"Well, when I told her she snapped at me. Here's how it went."

"That's a lot of money!"

"I know Ellen, like I said you already do so much for me by opening up your home allowing me to stay here."

She took out her checkbook, and as she was writing the check she continued:

"You can't park on the driveway anymore, it's too dangerous."

"OK Ellen."

After thinking about for a while, I decided I couldn't accept the money, it was too much. I went to hand it back to her, telling her just that:

"Ellen I can't accept this. It's too much money. You already do too much for me."

"Are you sure?"

"Yes."

"OK well, I'll just leave it here on this bulletin board in case you change your mind."

"So now every time I come and go I have to stare at a check for twelve hundred dollars with my name on it as a broke graduate student."

"That's rough dude, sorry. You're going through a lot right now," John sympathized.

We plugged the destination into our phones and made our way in my Mazda Miata. There was a lot of accumulated snow on the ground, but the streets were clear, and it was an unseasonably warm Sunday afternoon in January. I looked forward to the Sunday drive aspect in my undersized sports car through mountain roads almost as much as the hike we were setting out for. We got a couple of miles away from John's newly purchased house before he exclaimed,

"Shoot, I forgot my sunglasses."

"Do you want me to go back for them?"

"Nah, thanks. I'll be alright."

"Hmm. I think I might have an extra pair."

I dug through the center console and located a pair I had been meaning to repair. I'd owned a couple of expensive sunglasses before but inevitably broke or lost those. Since learning my lesson, I would only purchase cheap sunglasses, with one of the benefits being when they broke I could replace them carefree.

The reason I was holding on to this pair planning to repair them was because they had been my grandpa's, and he had passed away just over one year ago. Not wanting for anything of his besides a few pictures, my grandma insisted I go through some of his things to just see if anything caught my eye. In doing so, I came across some vintage sunglasses that called out to me. I wore them so much that one of the nose pieces broke off.

Not wanting John to experience the pain or pressure of the metal piece digging into his nose, I handed John the sunglasses I was wearing and slid on my grandpa's for the first time in months—sure I should have had them fixed in that amount of time, I'm still working on my procrastination habit—I swear!

We got close to our destination, but as neither one of us had been to this area before, we got a little lost. This was back in 2011, and cellular service wasn't as good as it is today, and on top of that, we were in the middle of the woods. John doing his best to work with what we had, had both his and my smartphone on his lap each taking their place on either leg. Unable to get full service to decipher our best course of action, we decided to pull over and perhaps, with each of us working on our own phones independently with the intermittent service, we would have more luck. I noticed a rest station up ahead.

"I'll pull in over there to help you get our bearings."
"Sounds good," John agreed, without looking up from his lap.

Forty-three

Everything's Different Just Like That

Millisecond 1: *What the fuck is happening?*
Millisecond 2: *You're in a car crash.*
Millisecond 3: *How is that even possible? I did everything right.*

A car accident is an incredibly violent thing. How can a sentence be simultaneously cliché and a massive understatement? Time slowed down allowing for those

154

split-second thoughts to enter my mind. After the realization that I was in the car accident, the screeching of the tires pierced my thoughts and time sped back up. One interesting feature of this car accident was that there was no early warning of tires screeching or anything else for that matter. I have since learned that the blindsiding feature of this crash likely forestalled a life-threatening injury. The logic flows from the idea of injuries worsening with awareness because of the afforded time opportunity to tense up before impact. By being unaware and "loose" as a result, the body could dissipate kinetic energy more efficiently; much like how a boxer rolls with a punch instead of standing unwaveringly at the point of impact. Well, that's one good thing.

With time sped back up, I became aware of things as they were happening. The windshield shattered, and we were showered in glass. We were sliding sideways, and it seemed like an eternity before we came screeching to a halt. Instinct kicked in, and my paramount concern took over my entire consciousness.

"John, are you okay?!"

It felt like five minutes before John answered, even though it was probably just about five seconds as he did a body scan before answering.

John spit out a mouthful of glass. "Yeah, I think I'm okay."

I cannot express to you the sense of relief that washed over me in that moment. There simply aren't words for it.

John then asked me reciprocally, "Are you okay?"

Ready to pop out of the car to see if anyone else needed help, I almost ignored John's question. It was only after learning that John was okay, and him asking me if I was, that my body let me feel what was going on. "No, I am not okay. My leg is broken. Call 911."

That was my best attempt at being stoic. It didn't last. Later it was reported to me by the medical professionals caring for me that a broken femur (thigh bone) is among

155

the strongest bones in the body, among the most difficult to break, and one of the worst types of physical pain a human can experience. If there is something more physically painful, I surely never want to experience it. As soon as my body allowed me to feel that intense pain, I began to cry. It wasn't a sobbing a cry. It was a type of cry I had never experienced before. It was as if two faucets had been turned on and a steady stream of tears ran from the ducts down my face so that it was impossible to distinguish drops from within the rivers. That pain put me in contact with something truly awesome. That pain taught me how we misuse the word awesome in the modern day. I was brought back to childhood in a way. We cry so much more in childhood because we are overcome with new experiences. I was given an insight by remembering through a channel we ordinary don't have access to, as to why it is we cry. We cry as a response when we don't know what to do in the light of feeling something so intensely.

Forty-four

Crossing Double Yellow Lines

When I told John I'd be pulling over to help him get our bearings. I was hyper-conscious of the surroundings because I was on an unfamiliar two-lane, twisty mountain road. The rest station was particularly well situated because the road had straightened out. I could see about two hundred yards beyond the rest station and no cars were coming. I was so hyper-vigilant that I noticed a pickup truck behind me about the same distance away as far forward as I could see. The rest station was acutely small with a small parking area, and for this reason, I made my intentions very clear. I activated my blinker earlier than I might in normal driving, slowed my car at a steady constant rate, and only then initiated my turn.

The man in the pickup truck behind me then crossed the double yellow line to T-bone me in the opposite lane of traffic. There was never ever any wheel squeal to warn me of the impact. I estimate the rate of speed in which he collided with me at about 50 mph.

Forty-five

The Scene

A shady character came up to the driver side of my vehicle and asked me some superfluous question.

"Does it matter?!" I snapped.

He shrunk away in response. I was in too much pain to deal with such stupidity. I found out later that it was the loser that hit me. Furthermore, I discovered later still how much of a loser he really was—he was an on-duty park ranger recently demoted to part-time status. Before that, he was a lawyer and a judge of all things. Seemed like he was hell-bent on destroying his own life and anyone unlucky enough to cross his path. Total loser. Like I said, I didn't have time for him. Not only was I experiencing among the most physical pain a human can experience, the nature of the aftermath of the crash was amplifying that pain.

The loser motorist was driving a Ford F250, weighing as much as 6,307+ lbs. The plus is because there was an aftermarket cable winch system affixed to the front of the truck (in front of the bumper). Said winch system was what slammed through my driver side door instead of the bumper designed to dissipate the kinetic energy in the event of a crash such as this. Instead all of that energy being dissipated; it had been concentrated through my driver side door and then through me—shattering me.

That little Mazda Miata was among the worst cars I could have been driving in the event of a crash with these circumstances. Miata's are among the smallest, lightest, and least-reinforced cars on the road. The flyweight weighed in at 2,299 lbs. At one third the weight of the "weaponized" truck—I never stood a chance.

Forty-six

Stop Talking

After the shady driver shrunk away, I was facing an immediate undertaking. My crushed-in door was pinning me between the twisted metal and my center console, amplifying the searing pain. I had no bullet to bite down on, but I steeled myself best I could. I placed my left hand on what was remaining of my door and my right hand on that center console. I took a deep breath and pushed hard both against the car and the mounting agony. With the pressure building on my already broken leg, the pain intensified exponentially. On the verge of blacking out, I pushed harder still, until I could feel my broken leg flexing, further signifying I was almost free from the pin. After one final exhaustive effort through the worst of the stabbing pain, I burst free. A sense of relief spiked through the pain momentarily. I went to relax by sitting back down, and that momentary relief quickly subsided back into excruciating pain. Turns out I would not be able rest on my injury or anywhere near it. I propped myself up with my upper body, alternating between using the steering wheel, center console, and passenger seat. I would have to do this for the hour it took for the proper first responders to arrive and extract me. People have since asked me if I went into shock as a result of the crash—I wish.

John had since exited the vehicle and attempted to call

911. He was still disoriented from the crash, and some nearby hikers came on to the scene.

"Hey, would you mind calling 911 for us?" John asked one of the hikers as he handed him my phone.

Side note: that hiker stole my phone—talk about insult to injury. It took the police about 10 minutes to traverse those rural roads to arrive on the scene. A female officer approached me to assess my condition.

"Hello there, how are you doing?"

"I'm in severe pain. My leg is broken."

"OK, the fire department is on their way with Jaws of Life to get you out."

"OK, good."

"Do you know what year it is?"

"2011."

"Good, and the month?"

"January."

"OK, do you know who the president is?"

"Obama. Listen I need pain medication."

"We cannot administer that until you're out of the car."

"OK, then I need you to stop talking to me so I can meditate to alleviate this pain the best I can."

"OK, well I'll be right over there. Holler if you need anything."

"OK."

As she was walking away, I went to readjust my grip because I was fatiguing in the position I was holding myself up in. For added leverage, I inadvertently grabbed the stick shift lever and pushed against it to carry my bodyweight. In doing so, I knocked the lever out of gear into the neutral position, and the car began rolling forward directly towards a ravine. The officer noticed the car headed towards the ravine and began running back towards me, screaming,

"Hit the brake! Hit the brake! Hit the brake!"

Trouble was, the way I was propping myself up I couldn't reach the brake. I let go of the shift lever, falling back down on my broken leg and through the blinding stars of pain, I was able to grab the emergency brake and pull it up just in the nick of time, averting careening down that ravine.

"You have to leave the car in park," the officer scolded.

I rolled my eyes around the pain stars and snapped back, "It's a manual transmission, and in the process of holding myself up off my broken leg I accidentally knocked the shift lever. I have since engaged the emergency brake. I intend to leave it engaged as I don't want to fall down that ravine."

Forty-seven

My Way on [or] the Highway

It took the fire department about 45 minutes to arrive on the scene with the proper tools including the Jaws of Life. I never learned why it took as long as it did for the fire department to arrive, but I can tell you when they did show up on the scene, a sense of calm rose up through the agony I was in, albeit briefly as that pain was really something else.

"We're gonna get you outta here kid."

"Thank you."

The firefighting team went into action with remarkable professionalism and efficiency. One cut open the hood to disconnect the battery. Another pulled all the fuses, and another cut the steering wheel to manually disable the airbag. They had doubled their redundancy to ensure that airbag didn't explode on my already compromised body. Next, they cut through the windshield and peeled back the roof like opening a can of sardines. They tried cutting through the mangled door, but it was fused from the crushing pressure. Realizing it would be easier to extract me up and out at this point, two of the firefighters jumped onto the wreckage of my once car. One was standing on the passenger seat and one standing directly over me, with the rest of the team encircling us, providing tacit support.

"OK guys nice and easy now," the team leader directed.

Before they even initiated their extraction, I was accidentally bumped by one of them, and the pain intensified through my leg like a lightning bolt strike, and I let out a massive howl. I didn't know it then, but when a bone as big as your femur breaks, it's not a particularly neat affair. Imagine if you were to break a 2x4 piece of wood over your knee; the aftermath would not look like you had neatly sawed the piece in two—it splinters, leaving slivers and shards at the edges. When the firefighter accidentally nudged me, the shards in my leg began to knock and rub against one another—spiking the pain to 11 on a scale of 1-10.

"Sorry kid, just trying to get a good purchase for the proper leverage to lift you out of this."

The firefighters took up their positions to lift me out. The one standing directly over me bent down to lift my upper body from underneath my armpits in the way one might lift a child. I could tell this was going to be worse than hellish. Instinctively I wrapped the firefighter over me in a wrestling hold and clamped down tight to bring our centers of gravity closer, decreasing incidental movement of my lower extremities.

"Son, if you hold me like that I won't be able to lift you out."

I imagine he must have felt how a water rescuer feels when a panicking drowning victim latches on. That survival instinct is a strong one.

"You *have* to lift me out this way."

While he had the support of his firefighting brothers to help lift me, the one standing directly over me had more than the lion's share of the lifting to do. And, like a lion, he found the strength to lift me in that compromised position.

"Watch his leg!"

"We got it."

And just like that, I was lifted by these firefighting heroes and delivered to the awaiting gurney.

"Thank you, guys. Thank you. Thank you. Thank you…"

Forty-eight

Beavis and Butthead

The firefighter handed me over to the two paramedics on scene, Bevis and Butthead. They struggled to figure out how to get the gurney into the ambulance. The same firefighter who found the strength to lift me in a manner he himself thought he could not, walked over to these two bumbling idiots. Despite it being the ambulance company's equipment, this hero firefighter was willing to undertake the simpler task of working the folding mechanism for the wheels that these paramedics couldn't figure out. With the firefighters' leadership, he and the paramedics lifted me into the ambulance. John hopped on to accompany me to the hospital.

"I need pain medication for my broken leg."

"We're working on it."

"Please, work on it faster."

One of the two geniuses pricked me with a needle and attached an IV bag to finally deliver that much-needed pain medication.

"We've got the morphine pumping. It shouldn't be long before it takes the edge off."

"OK good." After they secured the gurney, we left for the hospital 20 miles away. The lights and sirens were on full blast as we sped down the twisty and bumpy mountain roads. Over every single bump, I would get jostled, and the shards of bone that were once my femur would inevitably clash together, producing spikes of pain worse than the worst pain imaginable.

"Can you please slow down over those bumps?!"

"Just trying to get you to the hospital as quickly as we can."

"Does it matter if we get there five minutes sooner?! My leg can't take all the jostling!"

"OK fine."

Not even five minutes later, Butthead began strapping down my leg. All seemed well enough. But after, with no warning whatsoever, he began pulling my leg apart, causing my splintered femur to violently scrape against itself. This was the single most painful event I have experienced in my entire life.

"AHHHHHH!!! STOP WHAT YOU'RE DOING RIGHT NOW!" I roared.

"Your leg has to be put into traction!!!" Butthead screamed back in rebuttal.

"I understand that, but I *cannot* be conscious when that happens! I am a fighter, and when someone causes me pain, I redeliver pain ten-fold!!! If you try that again, I will break these restraints and then I will break you!!! Understand?!"

"OK fine. I'll let the emergency room personnel handle it—but if they ask why your leg isn't in traction I'm telling them you refused."

"I don't care what you tell them, just do *not* do that again."

Another ten or fifteen minutes went by and my leg was still in excruciating pain.

"Hey, I'm still in incredible pain. I need more pain medication."

"We've given you the maximum allotment of morphine permitted. We'll tell the emergency room physician you're still in pain."

After a little while longer, we finally arrived at the hospital in Suffern NY—how fitting, suffering in Suffern. Bevis and Butthead thankfully were able to manage getting the gurney out of the ambulance. Upon getting me out, Bevis lets out, "Oh shoot!"

He pulled a neck brace out of the ambulance.

"We were supposed to put this on you for the ride over. If we roll you in without this on you, we'll get in a lot of trouble. Can we put it on you now?"

"Yeah, I don't care. Can you just hurry up? I'm still suffering in pain."

Bevis pulled apart the Velcro, secured the brace around my neck, and then Butthead rolled me in.

Forty-nine

Smarty Pants

Bevis and Butthead handed me off the ER nurses.

"Hi sweetie, we're going to take good care of you," one of the nurses comforted me.

"OK thanks. I'm still in tremendous pain."

"OK I will let the doctor know. We will debrief the paramedics to learn what and how much pain medication they administered."

"OK thanks."

"Hang tight, hun."

The emergency room doctor came over and didn't even greet or acknowledge me.

"Hi doctor. I'm still in a lot of pain."

He didn't respond. He directed one of the nurses to cut off the rest of my pants (Bevis or Butthead had cut off my left pant leg already). The nurse complied, and I was now lying on the bottom of what was left of pants. The doctor walked back over and again, without saying a word, grabbed a hold of the pant material I was lying on and ripped it out from underneath me. I let out a scream almost as loud as the one back in the ambulance and followed it up with, "You couldn't have alerted me to what you were going to do?! You couldn't ask me to lean one way or the other so you could remove the material mitigating the pain?!"

"Sorry," he mumbled inattentively.

As this was all happening, there was a lady in the emergency room along with me. There was only a curtain separating us, and she was experiencing some sort of gastrointestinal problem. The entire time since I had been wheeled in, this poor lady was incessantly screaming bloody murder from the pain she was experiencing. This nonchalant doctor said to one of the nurses, "Can you please go and shut her up?" The nurse went over to comfort the lady. Now, I wasn't screaming my head off, but I was still in excruciating pain that wasn't getting taken seriously. I decided to change tack and tried to appeal to his intellectual side. I called on my rudimentary medical knowledge derived from my parents.

"Doc, now I'm merely a layman, but would an epidural work? I'm in a ton of pain and I just need to not feel from the waist down."

No response. Asshole. He left to go attend to another patient. Now as smart as one has to be to become a doctor, it doesn't necessarily correlate with bedside manner. Furthermore, there are different types of intelligence. For example, one might be bright enough to be a doctor but oblivious to social cues or even their surroundings. Say a man comes into an emergency room with a broken leg and his friend comes in with him to get checked out himself. The man with the broken leg might get checked out by a doctor, and his friend might get checked out by the same doctor. OK enough beating around the bush. Dr. Asshole walked next door where

John was being evaluated for any potential injuries. In front of John, Dr. Asshole mocked me to one of his colleagues.

"You won't believe it: the punk kid next door thinks he knows what he's talking about and suggested I give him an epidural," he snarkily scoffed.

Meanwhile, I led with my layman status and all I was trying to do was not feel the penetrating pain of a femur fracture. Asshole.

As it turns out there is a lucky subpopulation of people that are immune to morphine. Guess who one of the lucky winners is? Thankfully at some point, someone finally figured this out and were able to get me onto the pain medication Dilaudid, and for the first time since this whole ordeal began, the pain went from an 11 down to a nine. It's funny how a nine on the pain scale could be a relief.

Fifty

Re-redress

Shortly after receiving the second narcotic administration to my system, I was visited by a park police detective.

"Hey there, how are you feeling?"

"I've had better days."

"Yeah, I suppose that would be true. Listen, I'm really sorry I have to do this at a time like this, but I have to take your statement for what happened at the accident."

"Now?! I am still in immeasurable pain and have been administered narcotics by the first responders and hospital staff."

"I was sent here by my boss to take your statement. Please just do the best you can. You can dictate and I will write it down. Once you're done, you can look over what I record and then sign it."

I don't know how the hospital staff allowed this, or how they didn't provide me an advocate at least to help me through this. I did the best I could with what was being asked of me in the state I was in:

"I was driving on Seven Lakes Drive. I was lost and took a wrong turn. I was looking for a place to pull over and look at a map. There were no shoulders on the road. I saw a small building on the left side of the road with a shoulder. I slowed down, placed my blinker on, was aware of a pick-up truck behind me, but far behind. I noticed there was no oncoming traffic. Then proceeded to turn onto the shoulder. The pick-up truck crossed over into oncoming traffic and slammed into me—driver's side, at a speed I estimate to be fifty miles per hour. I was startled and in a lot of pain. The driver side door crumpled in, pinning me to the center console. I feel lucid, but am under the influence of pain medication administered by the healthcare professionals and first responders."

The detective had me read it over and sign it. Through my foggy vision, I complied.

"Now listen, I hate to have to do this. Don't worry about it now, just focus on healing up," the detective said in a shameful voice. With that, he pulled out and issued me a prewritten ticket for an illegal U-turn I wasn't making.

"What?! I wasn't making a U-turn."

"You can dispute it in court if you'd like. Please read the ticket and then I'll need you to sign it. Signing it does not admit guilt, just that I explained it to you and that you understand."

I read over the ticket through my delirious drugged state, with the distracting pain still piercing and dominating my consciousness, and signed it. He then skedaddled like a sinner fleeing church, or like a park police detective covering-up for his loser park ranger friend.

Fifty-one

After the detective had left, I had my first moment to myself in the middle of this whole ordeal. Out of the corner of my eye, I caught a glimpse of something on my forearm. I quickly examined it further, fearing that it was blood. It wasn't. I had gotten my first and only tattoo a month earlier and still wasn't used to seeing it on my body. I had gotten the tattoo cautiously. I waited years after wanting it before making the commitment to voluntarily, permanently altering my body to ensure it wasn't a fleeting whim. The tattoo was two Japanese Kanji characters (押忍) that combined to make one-word: Osu, or Oss, pronounced [oʊs]. The characters themselves mean to push (oneself) and to endure. The word is closely connected to martial arts study and practice and encapsulates several related meanings: being present in the moment, doing the best you can even when things are going wrong, patience, determination, and perseverance to name a few. The reason I had chosen my forearm for the tattoo was so that I would be able to see it and be reminded of the message. For that same reason, I had gotten it right-side up for me and upside-down for everyone else.

One of the reasons I held off for years before going ahead with getting the tattoo was because it was against the Jewish faith. With the somewhat unique upbringing of my dad being Jewish and my mom Catholic, they had both agreed to raise my siblings and me as Jewish. Without going too far into the weeds of my religious teachings—we were not a particularly religious family, however many of the morals and ethics learned from religion were of the utmost importance in our household. I even studied philosophy as an undergrad to further educate myself in ethics and morals to help me understand and then lead a good (if not better) life. My dad was pretty insistent we were brought up Jewish, but we sort of cherry-picked how we observed. For instance, we didn't keep kosher. Boiled down I didn't view not keeping kosher as immoral nor getting a tattoo.

My dad on the other hand, while choosing not to keep a kosher house, had a strong opinion on the whole tattoo thing—go figure. I called him up to deliver the news before I would see him at the winter holidays, Hanukkah and Christmas (we'd go to my Grandparents' for the latter holiday) in the hopes it might soften the blow. I prefaced dropping the bomb by emphasizing that I had made a personal decision.

"Dad I have something to tell you that may upset you, but I just want you to know I made a decision that is important to me and not in any way acting out of rebelling or anything of the sort."

My dad got curt on the phone, sensing the impending bad news he was about to receive.

"OK so what is it?"

"I got a tattoo related to my martial arts that offers me meaning beyond that."

"OK," he answered, unsuccessfully trying to cover up his disapproval.

"OK? Are you upset? Do you want to know any of the details about it?"

"I'm not thrilled about it, and no not really—I don't care to know anything else about it."

"OK, well I just wanted to tell you so you might not be as upset when you see it."

"I understand...so you got it already then?"

"Yes Dad," I half-laughed as I answered.

"OK then. Well I guess I'll see you at the Hanukkah party."

"OK Dad. Sorry if this is upsetting, but this is something very meaningful to me."

"I understand. I'll talk to you later."

"Goodbye Dad."

I couldn't have known when I was getting that tattoo just how meaningful and inspirational it would be. There I was, shattered, in unimaginable pain and the one and only tattoo I have, I received just one month earlier was staring me in the face. Telling me to endure and persevere.

Fifty-two

Confronting Mortality

Melissa, John's fiancée, had been the first warm and familiar face to make her way over to the hospital. She was visiting with John as I was going through all of the shenanigans with the pompous doctor and detective cuck. Afterward she came over to offer some comfort.

"Hey Dave, how are you feeling?" she asked as she delivered a gentle hug.

"Still in a lot of pain, but the pain medication is starting to take effect."

I'm not sure if it was because Melissa had become one of my very best friends and being in her familiar and consoling presence peeled away my defensive coping mechanisms or if it was that the awareness of her seeing me in that state was hard for her (she was fighting back tears), but either way this was the first time in the whole ordeal where the gravity of how close I came to losing my life sank in. I tried to express this thought to Melissa, but I couldn't get it out. I broke down. Similar to how the pain washed over me while I was still trapped in my car, the awareness of my mortality washed over me in that moment and completely overwhelmed me. I was trying to

170

convey that epiphany to Melissa, but the words got caught in my throat, and I couldn't choke them out. Melissa couldn't hold back her tears any longer—we cried together. I was still trying to share my realization with Melissa.

"That...could...have...been..."

Melissa cut me off. "It's OK. You'll heal up and be OK. You don't have to say it."

I took a couple of hyperventilated breaths, choked back some sobs and insisted, "That could have been it. I could have easily lost my life..." The most intense wave of guilt washed over me. "I have my entire life's work ahead of me."

"You're still here. You will do all those things you intend to do." She hugged me again, and we cried some more.

Fifty-three

Multi-tasking

John was getting evaluated in an adjacent room. He was diagnosed with a minor concussion and whiplash—a relatively auspicious outcome given the violence of the crash. My injuries were still undiagnosed at this point as the focus had been on pain management. Now that the pain was finally coming under control through medicines that actually had an effect, the doctors could then direct their attention to diagnosing the extent of my injuries. The first step of the process was for me to have x-ray photographs taken and to undergo an MRI. A couple of orderlies came to wheel my gurney to the x-ray and MRI machines.

As I was undergoing the imaging procedures, Melissa took it upon herself to call my parents to let them know what had happened. Hard as it was for them to learn of the circumstances, they were grateful for the call. I later learned Melissa's call was the only one my parents received about the accident. The hospital never reached out. My parents were a few hours away and immediately sprung into action. My brother was only 12 years old at the time, and my parents thought it best for him not to see me in the state I was in. They quickly arranged to have him watched by my gracious Aunt Kathie and Uncle Ralph. They dropped him off at their house a town over and then made their way over to pick up my sister who they had already relayed the news to.

The hospital was a few hours' drive away. Just so happened that all of the testing I was undergoing took about the same amount of time to complete as my family's drive. It couldn't have been more than 15 minutes from the time I was wheeled back to the emergency room to when my family was at my side.

My dad was first to make it by my bedside. With a concerned look on his face, he asked, "Are you in a lot of pain?" While the newly prescribed pain meds had taken some of the edge off, I was still in incredible pain. Even still, it dawned on me I had a moment in time that I would never be able to get back. If there were ever a time where I might get away with a little more, it might be now. I moaned, and I groaned, and I slowly answered,

"Uh...yeah...." Then without skipping a beat, I sped up my speech, "but the tattoo's healing!!" With a smug smirk, I pulled my concealed arm out from underneath the sheets, exposing to him my new ink for the first time.

My dad didn't so much as even scoff or feign a truncated laugh. "Seriously. Seriously. Are you in pain?"

I laughed. "Yes Dad. My leg is broken. I am in a lot of pain."

I guess that didn't work. Well, maybe it was in my delivery. I dared one more time.

"You know Dad, I've been thinking. You really ought

to rest easy about the tattoo. I got the tattoo on the 'non-Jewish' half of my body. The Jewish half is still tattoo free!"

He rolled his eyes, ignoring my second attempt and asked, "Are the results from the testing in?"

"I don't know. They haven't told me anything yet."

"OK hang tight. I'll see what I can find out."

I'm no comedian, but come on—those jokes were at least a little funny right? Oh well.

Fifty-four

A Martial Artist is Born

As I mentioned earlier, I waited years to get that tattoo to ensure the best I could it wasn't a fleeting whim. To offer a sense of scale, I got that tattoo five years to the day that I became a martial artist, which also happened to be on my birthday. Side note: even though it was only two Japanese characters, I toured numerous tattoo parlors in New York City, and evaluated many tattoo artists work before landing on the genius I would allow to permanently mark my body. I am quite sure that what I asked for was far below the worth of this artist's time. His appointment book was so full that I had to book him months in advance just for two measly characters that didn't challenge him in the least. More sense of scale, I found out later that he was Rhianna's tattoo artist. Admittedly that's really just vaguely notable but should give a sense of how seriously I considered the decision.

The much more interesting story is how I became a martial artist to begin with.

Senior year of college I took a little bit of a lighter course load, and there was a physical education offering of personal defense taught by a married late middle-aged couple and co-owners of a local karate academy. They were a starkly unique-looking couple as the husband was a powerful but portly, black man with a receding hairline and spoke with a Caribbean accent. His wife was a rail-thin white lady with striking orange hair that was almost as long as she was tall (all 5'2" of her), complimented with distinctly thick glasses. Admittedly not a particularly great first impression, but they started the class with a few demonstrations and those more than made up for their frumpy appearances.

As the classes progressed, I became hungrier for more authentic and immersive martial arts study. Not only was I learning new things in the classes and taking to them rather quickly, seemingly simultaneously there was a rebirth of martial arts at the fringe of mainstream culture. It was the fall semester of 2005, and in the previous spring was the finale of the UFC's first-ever season of their popular reality show, "The Ultimate Fighter." To this day, many MMA aficionados proclaim that the final between Forrest Griffin and Stephan Bonnar was the best fight of all time. Some experts even go so far as to say that the fight was so good it saved the UFC altogether. Even all that notwithstanding, no one could argue that it brought martial arts much closer to the center of the mainstream. With the UFC's growing popularity, my friends, who ordinarily might not be so interested, had the fights on when I came over to hang out. We had a low-key night enjoying the fights with a few beers and the bug bit me. Thinking back to my high school wrestling experience coached by a national champion juxtaposed with what I was watching on TV and I blurted out, "I'm not impressed. I can do better than the guys we're watching." My friends busted up laughing. "Yeah. OK, Dave." Sure, I may have been fueled by the beers, but I meant it and decided then and there I would take the introductory karate class at my self-defense instructors' school. The alcohol also fueled my thoughts. *I'll show them.*

It was also around this time when I experienced the

first birthday of my life that I wasn't excited for. Twenty-two symbolized that I was getting older. Worse, the last few birthdays had so much to look forward to. At 16 I got my permit. At 17 I got my license. At 18 I became a legal adult. Sure, I had to wait few years from 18 to turn 21, but legally being able to drink was sort of a lot to look forward to, especially in our society. But 22? What's good about that? I'll tell you, nothing. Well, at least from a naïve 21-year-old perspective. As a result, I decided that I didn't want to celebrate this birthday. I told my friends numerous times to please not plan anything. I wanted to spend my birthday on my own. They all mockingly agreed, and I doubled down, imploring them. After all, it was my birthday, and I should be able to spend it how I liked, even if my circle didn't agree with me.

The day before my 22nd birthday I showed up to the karate academy and participated in my first official martial arts class. The instructors and students alike were extremely welcoming. I wasn't convinced because the meme of a traditional martial arts school of out of shape people "dancing around" was stuck in my head, and their intense enthusiasm came off as a bit cultish. That said, these seemingly out of shape people were able to perform movements and techniques I couldn't. I found it physically demanding, and the amount of focus it required really sucked me in. However, in line with that quasi-enthusiastic cultish feeling, I was picking up there was also a spiritual and meditative side to it as well. It was difficult to fully distinguish and identify if it all was hooey or authentic. But, I couldn't deny I had gotten something out of the class. So, what if people were friendly and maybe a bit nerdily enthusiastic—maybe that was a good thing. The class ended with everyone applauding my completion of the first class (admittedly a bit over the top, and contributed to my confused feelings on the whole experience). After the applause, the second highest ranking instructor (the rail thin, redhead with lengthy hair) concluded with an appeal to all the students.

"As many of you know this is our last class at this location. We are fortunate enough to be moving to a bigger and better location. We are starting early tomorrow morning as we have to be out by the end of the day per our lease agreement. Headmaster is actually at the new location now prepping it for all of our equipment to be moved. I hope to see all of you tomorrow. Osu?!"

The class responded in unison, "OSU!!"

The stern but friendly ginger karate master came over to me as everyone was packing up and put her arm around me.

"Well what did you think?"

"It was really great. Thank you for the invitation to come."

"You're most welcome. You are a natural. You have a true fighting spirit. I know this was only your first class, and I was speaking to the rest of class about volunteering tomorrow—they've been with us for years. You're welcome to come, but please don't feel obligated."

"OK, thanks again for the class."

I was glad to not be pressured to help after only my first class. It was a lot to take in, and I wasn't quite sure if it was right for me or not. While friendly, there was a bit of a nerdy affect to the atmosphere, and I was still early on in controlling my ego after years of trying to distance myself from a nerdy persona. I thought that this might be a step backward for me. Still, I didn't want to celebrate my birthday. I wasn't convinced my friends would honor my request, and no one here would know it was my birthday if I spent the day with them helping. And I guessed I could counteract my sulky attitude by being useful on that day. As I was drifting off to sleep that night, I convinced myself I would help volunteer.

Fifty-five

Sage's Wisdom

I woke up earlier than I would have usually on the weekend, especially on my birthday. I had a purpose today and the day was bigger than me and my silly unwanted birthday. The day was particularly cold, snowy, and grey. It seemed fitting. I took a shower to help me wake up, made some coffee, and got out the door.

I arrived at the old dojo where the master and his wife were loading one of their cars. Mary came over to me.

"David! So glad to see you! We're just loading up what's left here to take over to the new academy. Thanks for pitching in!" She gave me a big hug.

The master was inside on a ladder, uninstalling some lighting and fixing up some electrical work.

"David-son! Glad to see you! You can start over there and help Sensei Mary load up the cars." He pointed to one side of the room with his chin as his hands were occupied.

I began carrying various items to the car all the while making small talk with the Master and Sensei. After about an hour had passed, it was still only about eight in the morning.

I asked, "When is everyone else going to get here?"

The master shrugged with a hint of embarrassment and disdain. "They knew we'd be here at six this morning."

I decided to not to mention it again. A few more hours passed, and it was time for lunch. They were gracious enough to buy lunch from the local deli. I tried to pay for it, but they wouldn't have it. It was still just the three of us. Over lunch, they were asking me questions to get to know me better. Sensei Mary didn't eat much and got up early to get back to work as there was still a lot to do. She insisted that the Master and I sit, eat, and enjoy. With Mary whirling around moving objects out to the car like she was exquisitely performing one of her Katas, I labored to continue the conversation with the Master. His conversational skills were better than mine much like his martial arts.

"Sensei Mary tells me you had your first karate class yesterday, and that you're a natural."

"Gee she said that? I hope she isn't overstating it."

"You are too modest. I saw you in the self-defense class. You have real skill and potential."

"Thanks." I offer up my gratitude as I painfully and consciously work on taking compliments better.

I decided to float a line of conversation myself. "You know, my first ever martial arts class was the last class taught in this academy."

"Mmph! There's meaning in that," he grunted as only a true master could.

I contemplated whether or not to tell him it was my birthday, potentially adding to the meaning. I decided not to. They were already overly grateful, and I didn't want them to feel guilty about my decision to come help.

"Now come. Let's finish up. We still have a bunch to do, and I don't want to keep you too late."

We finished loading the cars, drove over to the new bigger and nicer dojo, and unloaded. We repeated that pattern several times until we had successfully loaded up the last of it. We swept up the old place and headed over to the new school one last time.

We unloaded the cars, and they offered to buy me dinner, but I graciously declined. It was fairly late, and I was tired after a full day of moving. They thanked me profusely before setting off. As tired as I was, they must have been even more so—I was about half their age, and we all had been working all day. I thought to myself I was really glad I had decided to come. I was the only one of their students to volunteer, and we were just barely able to get it all done after putting in a full day's worth of work. Furthermore, there were some pretty heavy objects that needed to be moved and had I not shown up, I don't think they would have been able to move them. After they thanked me once more, I set off for home.

Feeling less sorry for myself on this birthday, I ran over the master's words once more. *Mmph! There's meaning in that.* I didn't know it then, but that would be the day I would decide to become a martial artist—all on a birthday I didn't want. Five years to the day, I got my tattoo (押忍, OSU) on my 27th birthday, further making the commitment to martial arts. One month later, I was looking down at that tattoo in the hospital bed reading the message to endure and persevere. If that's not meaning, I don't know what is.

Fifty-six

Common Sense is Uncommon

My dad came back after speaking with the panel of doctors reviewing my x-rays and MRI. He didn't have an uplifting expression on his face.

"What's the story?" I asked.

"Your femur is broken as you expected. You also have multiple breaks all about your pelvis. It looks like five in total, one being down the center of your sacrum."

My heart sank lower than what I thought was already the bottom. To put the pain of a broken femur in perspective, it was so intense that it obscured five breaks in my pelvis. I would come to learn that the broken femur wouldn't permanently cover up the pain of the pelvic breaks.

"What now?" I ask in a crushed tone.

"Your leg needs immediate surgery. They are prepping the operating room right now. It is unclear if you will need any surgeries for your pelvis at this time."

I was wheeled out into the hallway in front of the nurses' station awaiting the signal to be transported to the operating room. Both my parents, my sister, John, and Melissa were all by my side. My dad was still talking with the doctors, collecting as much information as he could. My mom would transition from doing her best to comfort me and put my mind at ease and observe the medical professionals' conversation about the best course of actions for my injuries. This was the first time John and I were able to really talk to one another since this whole thing happened. Despite the fact neither of us had much to say, we had been friends for a long time, and we didn't need words. With John by the side of my gurney, a nurse had come over with all my belongings, including my clothing that had been cut off me, in a bag. The nurse took the bag and dropped it on my broken leg. I cried out in agony. Now it was John's turn to flip out.

"What the fuck is your problem?!"

"What? I didn't want him to lose his belongings."

"SO YOU DECIDE TO DROP IT ON HIS BROKEN LEG?! HOW THE FUCK DO YOU HAVE A JOB HERE?!"

The nurse shrunk away, as the rest of our party came over to see what all the commotion was about. John explained what had happened, but there was nothing to do about it after the fact. Chalk it up to just one more thing out of our control.

Fifty-seven

Out of My Hands for Now

I was wheeled down to the entrance of the emergency with my de facto entourage in tow. When we reached the doors of the operating room, we were greeted by the surgeon. A handsome young doctor, charismatic and caring. Dr. Popowitz told my friends and family that this was as far as they could follow me and to say their goodbyes. *Their goodbyes?!* He corrected himself. "Goodbyes only until the short routine surgery is completed." One by one each member of my support group hugged me and told me some variant of how everything was going to be OK, most of them fighting back their own tears. Dr. Popowitz asked us if we had any questions. Everyone in the party collectively shook their head.

"I have a question, doc," I piped up. "I am a martial artist and a fighter. Am I ever going to be able to fight again?"

I could feel the crowd wince at my perhaps too honest and premature question. Doctor Popowitz took it in stride. "Yes, I don't see why not."

The group let out a communal sigh, but I wasn't sufficiently satisfied.

"Doc, just to be clear. The upper thigh is a target in MMA. Opponents kick full force to that area."

I could still sense the group's apprehension revolving around my questions, but I had to know what to expect.

Cool as a cucumber the doctor paused for a moment to think, and offered up, "Yeah, I don't see it being an issue."

He could have taken the safe route and said he wasn't sure. He could have reflexively answered to assuage any fear I might have before a major surgery, but he didn't. He did the hard, honest work of really listening to my question, assessing it, and answering both honestly and reassuringly. Finally, a healthcare professional with good bedside manner.

"OK, I'm ready."

If most of my experience to this point since the crash was dealing with the junior varsity B-team of healthcare professionals, now in the operating room I was surrounded by world champion professional athletes. I later found out my analogy wasn't far off. Turns out Dr.

Popowitz was an assistant team physician for the Florida Marlins professional baseball team (now the Miami Marlins). Talk about being in good hands and prayers being answered. It did feel like a team of angels in there. They comforted me and assured me everything would turn out well.

"OK honey, we're going to start the process of putting you under. Next thing you'll know is waking up after being put back together," one of the nurses reassured.

"Glad to hear you all are better than all the king's men."

She smiled a courteous smile. "Count down from one hundred for me, hon."

I said a prayer. *Please God, look over me so I am able to fulfill my life's work of helping people.*

"One hundred, ninety-nine, ninety-eight…"

Fifty-eight

Kansas No More

The next thing I knew, I woke up all woozy, but put back together. My prayer had been answered. It felt as if my grandpa and my buddy Nick, who had both recently passed, were looking over me along with my other loved ones who were looking down on me. It was then when I remembered that I had been wearing my grandpa's sunglasses in the accident. It was as if those glasses were some sort of protective cloak, shielding me from even more serious injury.

I had tubes and wires going in and out of me from all sorts of places. I wasn't aware of any of that though. I was wrapped up in a number of heavy blankets, extending from my head to my toes. I was in the recovery room awaiting my vital signs to stabilize before I would be moved to a more conventional hospital bed. Looking up from my bed still in my quasi-dream state, I was surrounded by loved ones. Mom was there. Dad was there. Cindy was there. Even John and Melissa were there. It did all sort of feel like a dream, and it required intense labor just to speak. Everyone was dissuading me from talking, but I had something important to say:

"Someone ...take ... a ... picture ... of ... me."

Even in my delirious state, I knew a picture of me laid up like this on social media would be sympathy gold with the ladies. Everyone laughed in disbelief, reassuring me that it wasn't important, but I insisted, and they thankfully acquiesced if only for me to stop laboring to speak so my vitals could stabilize. Melissa pulled out her phone, told me to say, "cheese," and snapped the picture of me with a drunken half-smile, betraying just how proud I was of myself recognizing the opportunity. Sufficiently humored, everyone (gently) hugged me goodnight.

Fifty-nine

Bedside Manner Matters

The sleep I had after the surgery was the best I would have for a long time. It was the combination of all the anesthesia mixed with the longest day of my life. It would be months before I got another full night's sleep again. The main reason for that was all of the breaks encircling my entire pelvis. The *only* position where the pain wasn't excruciating when I was in any lying or seated position was dead on my back—and even then, it was only a couple of notches below excruciating. Wouldn't you know it that the only position I couldn't sleep in was on my back. I just kept winning the lottery.

That next morning, I was greeted by my mom and

sister who stayed the night at a local hotel. They asked how I was feeling.

"Shattered." In more than one sense. My heart had already begun to harden and fill with rage.

"I will make the asshole who did this to me pay."

My mom as the wise, compassionate, and competent woman she was said, "OK honey, we'll cross that bridge when we come to it."

That's all I could think about though as I lay there with intravenous lines coming out of my arms, no less than five electrodes stuck to my chest connected to an EKG machine, nasal oxygen cannulas, and perhaps worst of all, a urinary catheter.

I will make this asshole pay, I thought to myself one more time.

That whole next day I was waiting for that godsend of a surgeon to make his rounds and share my prognosis. The day was marked by how many times I could push the button by my bedside and have it actually deliver opioid pain medication. The apparatus was set up such that it would only administer the medication once per hour, no matter how much pain I was in or how many times I pushed that small red button. Eight. It took eight successful presses (or eight hours if you're keeping up with the math) for the doctor to show. Only it wasn't Dr. Popowitz, professional baseball team grade as it were. Instead, it was one of his partners who I had no interaction with prior. Turned out Dr. Popowitz was called in for another emergency surgery. Dr. Substitute spent all of five minutes with us. Optimistic as I was given Dr. Popowitz's confidence and prediction going into surgery, I was eagerly awaiting the news I'd be able to bust out of that hospital joint in a day or so. In those five un-emotive minutes with Dr. Substitute, he all but laughed at my notion I'd be leaving the hospital so soon.

"Listen kid, I appreciate your enthusiasm, but you received some pretty serious injuries. Odds are when you have a single break in your pelvis it will either cause nerve damage or it will compromise the ability to weight-bear. You have five; you do the math."

Now, I had already taken two graduate level statistic courses—I knew the doctor was probably right about the probability, but I couldn't help but think there could have been a softer way to deliver that news. I guess he hadn't taken the courses in counseling I had, but still—bedside manner is a thing, right? It got worse.

"You're likely to be in a wheelchair for the next six months to a year," he concluded and promptly exited to get on with the rest of his rounds.

My sister and mom tried to console me. "That's just one doctor's opinion. Don't overvalue it. Dr. Popowitz will be in tomorrow morning to go over it in more detail."

I rolled over to not have to face them. I wasn't exactly in a glass-half-full sort of mood. That night I had my first restless sleep, and it would be half a year before I had a full night's sleep again.

The following morning Dr. Popowitz visited my hospital room. I was less affected by his cheerful demeanor, and he could tell.

"What's wrong?" he asked.

"Your colleague stopped by yesterday evening to let me know that due to so many breaks around my pelvis that I was likely going to be relegated to a wheelchair for the next six months."

"Yeah, he shouldn't have said that. He didn't perform the surgery and isn't as familiar with your case as I am. I am sorry for his words. Moreover, after carefully examining your x-rays and MRI scans I am confident you will be able to ambulate with a walker and/or crutches. There is a step-by-step procedure that the hospital physical therapist will walk you through; sorry, no pun intended," Dr. Popowitz explained.

"Dr. Substitute made mention that when one break happens in the pelvis it likely either affects nerves or the ability to weight-bear though," I protested unwittingly.

"While he was right about the odds of a break in the pelvis affecting either one of those two things, all five of your breaks do not compromise either the nerves in the area or your ability to weight-bear. I imagine it has a lot to do with the excellent physical shape you kept yourself in through the martial arts," Dr. Popowitz patiently and calmly explained.

My morale instantly shot up. Dr. Popowitz really was a godsend, and as if to solidify that thought, as he exited the room, he called back, "All of the partners in our group were reviewing your breaks and how remarkable they were. All non-articulated, in benign parts of the pelvis, and the break down your sacrum is perfectly symmetrical—none of us have ever seen anything like that in our over fifty years of combined practice. You're a miracle kid."

One quick word on some speculation I had after the accident as it related to my martial arts training. In training, we would absorb strikes to all areas of our body in addition to using our limbs to strike heavy bags and the like. This variety of punishment often causes micro-fractures in our bones, much like the act of working out (say through weightlifting) causes micro-tears in the muscle. In either case of the micro-fractures or micro-tears, both actually *weaken* the corresponding bone or muscle. Our bodies have an amazing ability though. Our body responds to this stress stimuli and grows back denser and stronger. Interestingly, my parents' main objection as healthcare professionals to my MMA training was all the punishment my body would take. It is impossible to prove that all that training sustaining micro-fractures allowed for my bones to grow back stronger, and in turn may have not only saved my limb, but also my life.

You'll remember the unpleasant image of a 2x4 broken over one's knee and all the splintering left in its wake was what my femur looked like. Well, had one of the splinters happen to severe my femoral artery (one of the largest arteries in the body) in conjunction with being trapped in my car for an hour—that could have been all she wrote. It scares me to this day how by the narrowest of margins (not more than a few centimeters) I could have bled out instead of writing this book. Side note: when my parents object to my martial arts training since the accident and I protest that it may have saved my life and certainly mitigated the already horrific injuries, they remain unconvinced.

Sixty

Skipping Steps

Even though my parents and I didn't see eye to eye on my martial arts training, we were all glad I had logged all those hours and taken all the beatings so my bones would grow back denser. And, despite my parents' chosen professions were contributing factors to our disagreeing, I have always felt incredibly lucky and secure to have a doctor and a nurse for parents. Perhaps never more grateful while I was lying in the hospital bed.

When one of the nurses came into my room to do various things about all the equipment I was hooked up to, I noticed my mom peering over her shoulder as she worked. At one point when the hospital nurse was fiddling with my IV bag, my mom asked a few questions having to do with the ratios of the fluids/meds in the bag. I could tell from the tone of my mom's voice that the nurse had done something wrong. My mom may have been asking questions as she phrased her words, but in reality, she wasn't asking any questions at all—she was as politely as she could informing the nurse she had the ratios off, or whatever it was (I'm not a nurse). The nurse paused and thought for a moment and responded to my mom.

"Gee, you're right," and proceeded to make the proper adjustment.

Once the nurse left, I looked at Mom in disbelief and asked, "What if you weren't here? I wouldn't know what she's doing."

My mom, cool as a cucumber answered, "Nothing to worry about. I am here."

"But, what *if* you weren't."

"We, can't play that 'what if' game. Nothing happened, no sense worrying about it."

Those were her words, but I'm pretty sure I saw her roll her eyes at the nurse's incompetence. Crisis averted by my Supermom.

My mom is not only a nurse—she is many things to many people. Growing up, she worked as a lifeguard, and later in her life I would witness her actions as a child. Our family was on vacation one summer in Maine. I must have been about seven or so, making my sister Cindy about six. We were playing in the pool, and my mom was watching us from just outside the pool. Without warning, my mom sprung to her feet and entered the water with the most graceful of dives. As she surfaced, she brought up a small child, no older than three from the bottom of the pool. The child scared, and not knowing my mom started crying and calling for her mom. The small child's embarrassed parents thanked my mom profusely.

"Thank you! Thank you! Thank you! I just turned away for a second. Oh my God this could have been so tragic!"

"You're welcome. Relax, stay calm. Everything is ok; nothing happened. Just let this be a lesson that it only takes an instant with kids and water for things to turn south," my mom soothed in that same voice I was hearing in the hospital room.

My sister and I witnessed the whole thing at young and impressionable ages, and for the remainder of our vacation my sister would drift out a little too far beyond her comfort, and I would swoop in to "save" her, like two cubs playing and acting out what they learned from their momma bear. Of course, all this was in our imaginations. My sister was never in any real danger, and I never really saved her. All of this was happening under good old mom's careful and watchful eye.

Not to leave my dad too far out of this, I look up to him too. I remember being in awe learning of some of the ways he was able to help people and save lives in his job. All of that combined with learning on more than one occasion that Mom and Dad, "off duty," happened upon emergencies and performed CPR when duty called without warning. Looking back, there was little doubt where my sister and I acquired the ability to act in a crisis like in that water rescue. My parents were still acting as my heroes even as an adult.

Sappy stuff aside, I now needed to learn how to bust out of this hospital joint. In order to be discharged from the hospital, I had to demonstrate proficiency and autonomy to the resident physical therapist. He briefly stopped by to set up an appointment for the following day to start showing me the techniques I would need to get out of bed, go to the bathroom, use a walker, use crutches, traverse stairs, etc. Dr. Tall arrived and instantly saw the overzealous glean in my eye. After setting up the session for the following day, he was quick to temper my expectations.

"I can see you're a bit eager to get out of here. I will make you a deal: I won't hold you any longer than we need you here, but you have to trust my judgment to keep you safe. Even if it's to protect you from yourself," he kidded and winked.

"Deal!"

"OK, to start I want to set appropriate expectations. It doesn't always have to happen in this way, but nine out of ten times it does: first step is working with us here in the hospital, the next step will be to transfer you to an inpatient physical therapy ward where you can continue to practice and develop the skills we'll begin teaching you here, followed by outpatient physical therapy—similar to inpatient except you'll be cleared to come to and fro to the PT, and the final step will be you will no longer need the PT, and you'll be cleared to get around all on your own."

"I'm a little confused doc. The orthopedic surgeon said I was going to have wait months before I could even weight-bear on the broken leg. How am I going to do all that before I can weight-bear?"

"I'm sorry for my lack of clarity. This physical therapy has nothing to do with rehabbing your broken leg, yet. That will come. The orthopedic surgeon is a hundred percent right. You are to stay off that leg at all times. I'm here to teach you how to get around without the use of that leg. Additionally, I will be giving you techniques on how to protect that leg and the breaks about your pelvis. Last thing you want is to suffer a fall and knock the breaks out of alignment."

"Ah I see. Well, I'm eager to get this process underway. See you tomorrow!"

"I could tell! See you tomorrow!" the head doctor of physical therapy chuckled.

The following morning after dry eggs and soggy cereal the hospital served up for breakfast, I was given just that bit more of motivation to break free from this place. Generally speaking, time moved slowly in the hospital (especially since I didn't have my phone after that hiker stole it. You can probably tell I'm not still salty about that). I was thankful to have visitors when they came. Also, thankful that my mom brought my laptop so I could correspond with professors about why I'd be a little late back to class, as well as showing friends and family on Facebook my most recent snafu. Even if you add in surfing the web and watching TV; all that only took up so much time. When alone I filled that space with a combination of thoughts: vengeance on the park ranger who hit me (after replaying the crash in my head a few hundred times I was sure the only way the crash was even possible was only if he was texting or if he was drunk). The vengeance in my imagination took many forms, but mostly I wanted to be locked into an MMA cage with this guy who was a foot taller than me and 75 lbs. heavier. I would have given anything for that to be the focus of my upcoming physical therapy session. Realizing that reality would only exist in my imagination, I brought my focus back to reality and what I could actually do to make him pay. That's it, literally—I'll make him pay. I directed all of that energy into the procedures of suing someone. Lastly, I focused on my new path, with the end goal of healing to the point where it was no different than before the accident, and that meant I would have to fight again.

Dr. Tall walked into my room with a welcoming smile.

"Are you ready?"

"As I'll ever be."

"OK then, I need you to sit up and dangle your legs off the bed."

Man, he's talking as if that will be a difficult task. I've been an athlete in one form or another my whole life.

"Doc, I decided I'm fighting again real soon. No need to baby me through this."

"OK OK tiger. No doubt you will, but let's learn how to do everything properly so you don't have a silly injury pushing back that big fight of yours."

I went to sit up, and I couldn't believe how weak I felt. It had only been a couple of days of being laid up. I was lying down in one position the whole time sure, but it had only been for a couple of days. Also shifting my weight around my pelvis sent lightning bolts of pain shooting outward from it and radiated through the rest of my body. I did my best to not let the pain show on my face nor the struggle it was to merely sit up. My mom and the physical therapist did their best to remain stoic as well, but my pain and struggle was too great and my expression betrayed my pride, and in turn I could read on their faces a combination of their sympathy and professional concern. They didn't baby me though. Good thing because I would have had none of it. Slowly and carefully manipulating my weight with the most precision and concentration on what made my breaks hurt worse, carefully navigating away from those lightning bolt signals, I was able to sit up and dangle my legs.

"Great job!"

I was no longer appreciating the kind physical therapist's cheerful optimism, but I put up with it because I knew it came from a good place.

"Now don't get too upset. It's just a starting point, and I won't hold you back from what you're capable of. We'll advance as quickly as safety will permit."

I had no idea what he was talking about. Sitting up now, I responded with only a quizzical look. Dr. Tall stepped out of the room into the hallway to retrieve a walker that was carefully hidden out of my line of sight. He brought it into the room and reiterated, "It's just a starting point."

Great. I will literally be getting around on an old fogey walker.

I fought my ego back. *He's right, it's just a starting point!*

My ego knew it to be true but offered up one subtle protest before retreating. *It even has the damned tennis balls on the bottom.*

Dr. Tall piped up, breaking me from my own inner dialogue with myself.

"Slowly and steadily scoot yourself as far as you can to the edge of the bed and rest your good leg on the floor." He had a more serious tone now.

Weight-shifting my way forward through the agony, I achieved what felt like summiting a mountain—took me nearly as long too.

In that same serious tone, Dr. Tall commanded, "Before reaching for the walker, slowly stand on your good leg holding on to the bed for balance and stability."

"Just like that? Just trust all breaks in my pelvis will

hold?"

"Dr. Popowitz is the best in the biz. He said your pelvis is strong and stable. When you're ready, stand up."

I pushed forward and slowly started placing more weight on my good leg. I could feel strain in each one of the five fractures as they were being stressed. I pushed forward, trusting the team of people around me. I gritted my teeth through the pain and allowed it to drive me up to stand for the first time since I had been shattered—while still shattered. I *chose* to be strong. I *chose* to stand. I *chose* that this would be the first step back to full health marked only by winning another MMA contest. And after I chose to stand despite my crushed body warning me not to, I stood.

"Good work. Now, grab ahold of that walker one hand at a time. Once you have your balance and sturdy grip, you can carry your weight with your upper body as you swing your lower body forward," Dr. Tall instructed.

I took to it no problem. After that, the physical therapist kept to his word and kept challenging me. First to sit in an armchair that I sunk into, to be sure I could get up out of that. Next, to try crutches. Check and check. He was amazed at the control I had over both apparatuses. While my sister was the gymnast of the family, I too did gymnastics for seven years, which helped acquaint my body to the devices and more generally aided with my athleticism in all other sports I had done. Using equipment like the rings and parallel bars came back like riding a bike. I'm sure being on crutches for a broken ankle and countless sprained ankles also helped. Who'd have thought weak ankles would come in so handy?

Blown away by my natural proclivity to picking up the walker and crutches, Dr. Tall saw it fit to administer my final test: negotiating stairs. He walked alongside me down a long corridor. I thought he was taking me to the hospital staircase, and while tired, I was determined to conquer it. We turned the corner revealing a mock set of stairs comprised of wood with a light stain finish. The "staircase" was barely that as it only had five steps. I thought it was silly to have such a staircase when the hospital surely had their own functional sets. To be fair, they constructed this one with wide steps, a sturdy banister, and non-slip surfaces. After being taught the technique, I climbed and descended the stairs with ease.

"Well Dave, you have completely blown me away with how you've been able to negotiate everything thrown at you. Given the severity of your injuries and how recently you sustained them you shouldn't be able to do all you've done. I can honestly say I've never had a patient be able to do all you could so close to sustaining their injuries. I've never made this recommendation, but you have my approval to be discharged, skipping the inpatient and outpatient physical therapy steps. Keep up that determination young man."

Sixty-one

Jailbreak

Having flown through all of my PT requirements, I was eager to get out of that hospital bed and back to classes. I was one semester away from earning my masters and as it stood if I didn't make it back for this semester I would have to wait an entire year to take the required classes that only ran in the spring semester. It's a funny thing to call it a spring semester when the majority of it happens in the winter, or at least in winter weather. This year in particular was one of the snowiest winters in recent memory. It stands out to me for a number of reasons. Perhaps most prominently being just after achieving my hospital departure, a nor'easter rolled in, and I was holed up for an extra few days in the hospital. If you think cabin fever is an unpleasant thing, allow me to tell you hospital fever ratchets it up a few degrees.

Those few days eventually passed, and the roads were plowed. It was really time to go home. Well, to my parents' home, the home I grew up in. Two floor nurses came into my room particularly cheery that morning, excited for me that I'd be discharged.

"We have just one minor procedure left to do before we clear you. We have to remove your catheter."

"Oh man," I muttered.

"Remain at ease sweetie; it won't hurt. You'll just feel a slight pressure."

Sparing you most of the procedure, the nurse was now at the stage where she would be pulling the tube that extended into my bladder through my urethra.

"OK hun, try to relax. This will just take an instant."

She pulled with one swift continual motion.

Just a slight pressure?! My ass! Well my dick actually. I let out a piercing howl as I could feel every inch of the catheter being pulled out as if I was being ripped apart from the inside out of a rather sensitive area of the body.

The second nurse said, "Oh, come on don't be such a baby."

My eyes widened to express, *Excuse me, do you have any idea what it feels like to have something ripped through the inside of your penis?!*

Just as I was about to give her a piece of my mind, the first nurse piped up. "Oh no, I forgot to deflate the balloon."

There is a balloon that gets inflated in the bladder after passing through the urethrae. The procedure is reversed to remove it. The balloon is deflated, and then extracted. Well, at least that's how it's supposed to go.

That second nurse all of sudden had more sympathy for what I had just endured. As if I hadn't endured enough. It got worse. That still inflated balloon cut me on the tip of my penis. I couldn't piss straight for a month. I would have to sit to pee, and if that was emasculating enough—remember all those breaks in my pelvis? Well, sitting on a hard-surfaced toilet was among the most painful things I would have to do on a daily basis—and now I was relegated to sit on that torture throne many more times per day. I cursed that nurse with every piss until that cut healed.

Thankfully my mom wasn't present for my latest injury. She was busy pulling the car around to the front circle. I was wheeled down in a wheelchair by a couple of orderlies, and when the hospital doors opened and I was hit with a blast of frosty winter air, the type of wind that might make you wince and cuss winter, I was filled with appreciation just to be able to be around to feel it.

With the help of my mom and the orderlies, we loaded the walker and crutches into the car. Then, they loaded me into the car, being mindful of all of my breaks. The seat was laid as flat as it would go to assuage the pressure and pain about my breaks.

My mom turned to me. "Ready to go?"

"Let's blow this popsicle stand!"

Mom put the car and gear and away we went. We made it to the parking lot exit controlled by a traffic light and waited for it to turn green. Similar to how I managed to skip a bunch of steps with PT requirements, I started rattling off all things we would need to do to keep the positive momentum. My mom reminded me it was a process and not to get ahead of myself, but I had a focus like I never had before. She was of course right as moms usually are. The light turned green and we set off, marking the beginning of my new journey. Just as we started rolling, a car came careening through the intersection, blowing a red light. My mom expertly slammed the brakes narrowly avoiding the speeding car.

"WHAT IN THE ACTUAL FUCK?!"

"We're fine. Relax. And don't curse."

"That would have been it. If he hit us in the state I'm

in, that would have been it."

"It didn't happen. Let's just focus on getting home safe." Mom got me home safe without further incident. She was the calm, cool, and collected one on the ride home, and with the mission complete and the cargo delivered—she lit up a cigarette. Ordinarily I would have given her some grief over it, but not this time.

Sixty-two

Mutant Status

Like a well-oiled machine, the people in my life snapped into action. My aunt's long-term boyfriend and surrogate uncle of mine, Anthony, was gracious enough to track down an inexpensive car for me. Friends and family visited me as I was laid up on my parents' couch (I had a bed there, but it was too firm for my breaks). My close friend Nick who drove through the night so he could make my fight and friend's wedding, brought me the best-selling journey-based book, *The Alchemist,* by Paulo Coelho.

"Dude, I love this book!"

"Oh man, I was hoping you didn't have it."

"Nah man, it's the perfect get-well gift. I actually lost my copy and this is *exactly* what I need."

While so blessed to have had so many visitors and well-wishers check in on me, there are too many to list. Not only am I sincerely grateful for everyone in my proverbial corner, their support made a direct difference in boosting my morale to tackle my greatest challenge yet.

Apart from resting and corresponding with my professors about my timeline as to when I would be able to get back to classes, I decided all on my own I would overload my body with nutrients to heal broken bones. While not a doctor, I am well aware that the attitude in which a patient brings to their condition affects the outcome. I would be tenacious in my healing and stack all of the odds I could on my side to make a full recovery as quickly as possible. While there is conflicting literature on the benefits and hindrances of dairy and bone health, I grew up with the slogan, "Milk does a body good." Furthermore, milk is loaded with calcium, and calcium is good for bones. That logic was good enough for me. Good thing I happened to like milk, especially when mixed with chocolate or strawberry syrup. Without exaggeration, I drank one gallon of milk per day.

My mom took the point position in caring for me. About one week had elapsed since she took me home from the hospital. It was time to travel the two-plus hours back to Dr. Popowitz's practice for a follow-up. The purpose of this appointment was to x-ray all the breaks and the hardware put in me to make sure nothing shifted out of alignment. A titanium rod was inserted down the center of my femur, and three titanium screws held it in place. Amazingly, despite the rod being over a foot and half in length, modern technology had it so that I was only left three tiny scars less than an inch each. That internal fixation supported my leg well enough, so no external cast was needed. I was grateful that no surgery was needed for the breaks in my pelvis.

Dr. Popowitz greeted me with that same sincere warmth.

"You're still amazing me kid. After reviewing the new films from today, your breaks are already showing active bone growth. It's only been a week and there is no way we should already be seeing this. I didn't believe my own eyes and ran it by my colleagues. They confirmed both seeing the bone growth, and were equally baffled with what they were seeing. They kept asking me your age. Your bones are growing faster than a two or three-year-old with active bone growth. They couldn't believe you were twenty-seven."

I explained to him all of the milk I had been drinking and asked if that could be the difference maker. He thought for a moment much like when I asked him if I'd be able to fight again and shook his head.

"No, that doesn't really explain it. All the milk certainly isn't hurting anything, but something else is going on here. It's like you're Wolverine. Kidding aside, that positive attitude of yours goes a longer way to explain it. Additionally, all the hardware looks perfectly in place. You have my clearance to do it all. You can drive and you can go back to classes."

"Thanks Doc! I intend to be all healed next time I visit!" I joked back.

"Don't overdo it kid, but I don't think I'd be surprised by you anymore."

Mom and I set off after making my next appointment four weeks away. I had to admit I did like the Wolverine comparison. The quick healing was one thing, but the extra part of the analogy Dr. Popowitz and I both missed was that now my bones were even fortified with metal. Sure, it wasn't adamantium, but titanium was pretty damn close.

On the way home, I was in a pretty good mood, excited to start tackling all the logistics to finishing out my schooling. My mom was happy to see me happy. I owe her for all those long trips she took for me—really just a drop in the bucket for all of the other things she's done for me.

We started entering an onramp to the highway that happened to be of the particularly short variety. My mom, already a cautious driver, was extra cautious while transporting my broken body. She was eyeing a safe time to enter the highway. After about 10 seconds, the guy in the car behind us started to become impatient and began to aggressively honk his horn. My mom instinctively started to inch forward, but I could tell she was nervous and wasn't ready to go.

"Mom, relax. Forget about that jerk behind us. Go

when you feel ready."

"You're right," Mom agreed.

Just then the guy started honking even more aggressively this time, followed by him reaching his head out his window to scream, "Hurry up!"

My protective instincts took over, and I flipped out. I reached my own head out of the window to yell back, "Shut up! If you have a problem with how my mom drives, I will gladly knock you out. That way it won't bother you anymore!"

"Relax Dave! We don't need any more trouble," Mom scolded.

She was right that time. I was so angered by the perceived threat against my mom I had forgotten that I was shattered. Maybe I was still high on fantasizing about being Wolverine, but I was convinced I still would have found a way to kick that guy's ass if he continued to perturb my mom.

Sixty-three

One Hundred Dips On a Walker

We made it back home without further incident. I immediately called my cousin Eric to share the good news that I'd be heading back to New Jersey in a couple of days to finish out my degree. He was happy to hear from me and happy I was on the mend. I started working out some more logistical stuff when my phone rang. Eric had called back.

"Dave, I'm really sorry. I forgot that I'm going away for business this week."

"No worries cuz. I'll see you when you get back."

"I'm looking forward to it. Is there any way you can hold off a week yourself?"

"Classes are already in session. I just got cleared from the doctor. I'd like to catch up as soon as I can. Also, I have to take an additional class this semester that my cohort took over the summer when I fought. I was already behind before this damn car accident."

"Dave, I'm just going to be straight with you. Ellen doesn't feel comfortable with you being here in the shape you're in without me here."

"Eric, I can understand the concern, but I assure you I am a hundred percent self-sufficient. I am cleared to drive. I shower myself. I climb stairs by myself. I am a hundred percent good to go."

"OK Dave. I hear you. Let me talk to Ellen to convince her. I'll call you back." Convinced he'd be able to convince her, I got back to taking care of what I needed to. It was a whole hour before he called back.

"Dave, I'm really sorry." This time Eric said it with a defeated tone.

"I wouldn't lie to you, Eric. I am good to go. I swear."

"I know Dave. Ellen just doesn't feel comfortable without me here, and I can't convince her otherwise. I'm really sorry."

"Fine. Goodbye."

"It's just one more week. I'll see you soon."

"Right. Goodbye."

"I'm really sorry Dave. See you soon."

I went on some sort of cursing rampage in front of my parents. They insisted I calm down, but I wasn't calm. I was blinded by rage. My rage kept me from seeing Eric and Ellen's perspective. It prevented me from understanding that it was fear and not malice motivating their actions. Despite Eric and Ellen's default nature of generosity and hospitality, it was their fear of caring for a presumed invalid that created yet another obstacle for me.

After a few more shouted expletives and not knowing what to do with all this anger fueled energy, my body took over. Before I knew it, I started pumping out dips on my walker. One hundred of them. In all my working out, I had never done one hundred consecutive dips—and zero on a walker. I guess I had just never done dips while that angry before.

Sixty-four

Tumultuous Times

I was extra anxious to return and finish out my graduate degree as it symbolized a return to form after a serious academic stumble. I grew up a bit of a nerd. I can't help but think that part of the reason for being selected into the gifted and talented program by my second-grade teacher, Mrs. Greco, was because I had fooled her for the better part of the year. She had a two-bin system for distributing and collecting our work in the form of worksheets each day. As soon as we were done with our work, we were allowed to play with the toys and board games in the back of the room. I was the second one "done" every day. Hating jumping through hoops at such a young age, I mastered the skill of zoning out until that first student finally completed all of the assignments. Once done, he or she would place their work folder into the done bin and head to the toy chest, with me not far behind. Only, my worksheets would be completely blank. At the end of the day, I would go back to the done pile and covertly extract my folder, remove and discard the empty dittos, and place my folder in the bin ready to receive the next day's work. This went on for months. Whether or not you believe in karma, it's been my experience that none of us really get away with anything in the end. After those months had elapsed, Mrs. Greco finally realized she had no grades recorded in her grade book for me. My consequence? I had to give up my recess for the rest of the year and do that never-ending pile of dittos that had accumulated. Arduous and mind-numbing as it was, perhaps a small price to pay if it helped set me on the gifted and talented track.

Things were smooth sailing for a good while. I parlayed the gifted program into the honors and advanced placement (AP) track. I was successfully learning and competing among the best and brightest of our blue-ribbon school district. Though, by the time of my freshman year of high school I had begun to develop a bad habit—taking too many mental health days. Perhaps my parents were too lenient in the beginning. This allowed the habit to worsen. I became cavalier and would nonchalantly stroll down from my bedroom and pour myself a bowl of cereal as I told my parents I wasn't going to be going to school that day. What if there was a project due that I didn't complete? I would tell them to fear not, as I would take the day and complete it.

I had come to expect their rote response. "Dave, you can't keep doing this."

"I know. I know," I would placate them.

Smarter than I was mature, I was pretty happy with the arrangement. I viewed school as a waste of time because of course at the ripe old age of 15, I knew everything and I was smarter than all of my teachers. With the way things were set up, I was still maintaining good grades *and* I didn't have to go to school as often.

The beginning of sophomore year was when it all came to a crashing halt. There were some variations to my tactics. Sometimes I wouldn't miss school but would come in late after a class in which work may have been due. This was especially true during wrestling season so that I could still practice and compete even if I was delinquent in my academics—until one day when my parents had enough and my mom in particular decided to put her foot down.

"Mom, I'm going to need you to take me in third period today," I said nonchalantly.

"Not this time Dave. You go in now or not at all," Mom rebutted out of character.

"Don't be silly. I have work due second period, and neither one of us want me to get a zero on the assignment." A callous attempt at manipulation that ordinarily would have worked. Not this time though.

"Dave, I'm not kidding. Let's go now or not at all," Mom pleaded.

I laughed in response to show my disbelief that she'd actually follow through.

You might be wondering why I wouldn't want to take the whole day off. We were in full swing of wrestling season. Before I fell into my bad habit of missing school when I pleased, I played a game with myself—do the least amount of work to maintain good grades. It worked too well. On some level, it left me wanting to do hard work. Slacking off in wrestling was out of the question because I wasn't good. I had to bust my balls to merely keep up and stay on the team—and, only just barely. Only now was it obvious why I valued wrestling more than school—it was due to the fact that I was working hard at something. My aptitude for academics was far higher, and with little to no work, I had better outcomes than wrestling. I was moved by the challenge. My mom knew this and knew by denying me what I had been working for was the best way to affect any change in my behavior. Really my mom and I were locked in a battle for my autonomy and independence. For this reason, we were seeing one another as adversaries. My mom threw the first jab.

"One more thing: if you don't go to school right now it will be you who decided to not go to your wrestling meet."

"Yeah, yeah, Mom. I'll see you in a couple of hours when it's time to go," I said over my shoulder as I headed to my room.

It was a bit abrupt in how she decided to change her tune. I underestimated her seriousness, and she underestimated my stubbornness. Guess I was about to find out what happened when an unstoppable force met an immovable object. The time had come to leave to make it in for third period. I grabbed my bags and walked downstairs.

"OK Mom, it's time to go!"

"I told you I wasn't going to take you. You had your chance."

"Mom quit playing. Let's go."

"No. I'm not taking you."

"You made your point. I get it. Now let's go."

"No," and then she continued with a power punch following that earlier jab setting it up.

"And it was you that decided not to go."

Being the little wiseass that I was, I played it back at her. "If you don't take me to school right now, I won't go to school for a week. And it will be you that decided for me not to go to school for a week."

"No, I didn't decide that," Mom protested.

"Turnabout is fair play."

"Well I'm not taking you."

This time I could tell she meant it. I changed my tone from cavalier to pleading.

"Mom, I'm not bluffing. Please just take me to school. I won't miss any more school. I promise."

"Too late. I'm not taking you."

"Mom, I'll say it one more time: I am not bluffing. If you don't take me right now, I am not going to school for a whole week of school."

"I won't be coerced. You made your bed; now you have to lie in it."

"So be it."

I slowly walked upstairs back to my room. I laid my bags down at the foot my bed and laid myself down on top of the covers. I rested my hands behind my head as I stared up at the ceiling. The frightening, but clear thought flashed through my mind: *I've just started the third world war.*

Needless to say, that next week rolled around, and I

kept to my word. Trouble was, I was already running behind on all my work as you know of my nasty problem with procrastination. When I made it back to classes, every one of my seven or so teachers were breathing down my neck to make up all the work. Understandable perhaps, but none of my teachers were considering the other subjects and corresponding teachers that were pressuring me just the same with the work I owed them. As a result, I doubled down on my flawed strategy of skipping school to make up work, causing more pressure and fights with my parents and even more school missed. Cue the downward spiral.

Things devolved at an incredible rate. My parents and I were blaming one another. They saw me as a disrespectful, disobedient adolescent (which I was). From my perspective, they were simply in my way. As far as I was concerned I was still earning good grades; they just needed to butt out. I became so angry with their interfering and them ruining my life that I had no respect for them. Anger boiled over to the point that they could say anything to me and the only response I had for them was to look them dead in the eye and in a defiantly restrained, yet domineering tone utter, "Fuck you." They would tell me not to use such language, especially directed at them to which I replied a more forceful, *"Fuck you."*

The lowest things sank was when my dad had finally had enough. He came marching into my room and aggressively threatened, "If you're not going to go to school, then you're not welcome in this house!"

I laughed insolently in his face.

"That's it! Get out!"

With a quiet confidence, I tauntingly answered with two of the most insulting and challenging words. (No, not "fuck you.")

"Make me."

That was all my dad could take. Who could blame him? He lunged for me as to grab a hold of me and kick me out of the house himself. I locked up with him like two stags locking their horns. We were in a literal battle of dominance. After about a minute of throwing one another around, slamming into walls, but without throwing any blows, it was all over. After the dust settled, with my dad panting trying to catch his breath, he cursed me for being the disrespectful punk I was. While in the moment I was quite pleased with myself to have come out on top, I can see now that it wasn't a good thing for me in the long run. I was already arrogant, believing I was smarter than everyone around me. Mixing in my now established physical dominance at only 16 only served to feed my ill-formed ego.

Sixty-five

Chaos

I have one sister, Cindy, 15 months younger than me, and one brother, Travis, 15 *years* younger than me. Travis was born in the fall with a due date of two weeks before he was actually born. I remember really hoping he wouldn't be born on Halloween so that he could have the whole day to himself. Lo and behold, he of course was born on Halloween, and while he was growing up, we were able to tell him the whole world dressed up and went out to celebrate his birthday.

Now 15 years is quite the age gap, and needless to say, Travis was a bit of a surprise for the family. Turns out his All Hallows' Eve birthday dovetailed nicely with our corny parents, as they would go around saying, "Travis is our trick *and* our treat." He truly was a treat; he brought a new energy to the house and the love in our family grew. One small hiccup was that he was born with what was diagnosed as a sebaceous cyst: a common noncancerous cyst on the skin usually found on the face, neck, or torso. Travis' was just behind his ear.

A sebaceous cyst or so we thought. At three months old, Travis' pediatrician began to suspect the bump behind his ear was something else and recommended to my parents that they take him to a surgeon. The surgeon removed the mass, and it was sent out to pathology to identify what it was. The pathology lab couldn't identify what they were looking at and had it sent out to the United States Air Force Molecular Diagnostic Laboratory in Bethesda Maryland. After a few long weeks, the pathology diagnosis came in: Juvenile Fibromatosis. The down and dirty definition is a benign condition where connective tissue cells called fibroblasts proliferate in various tissues including muscle, tendon, ligament, and fascia. The lesions can enter adjacent soft tissues and can cause pain and/or disability. Additionally, this turned out be an incredibly rare disease. There were only 19 documented cases when Travis' was diagnosed. Needless to say, with a disease so rare, there was very little known about it, including best modes for treatment.

Six months later, the growth returned. Travis had another surgery to have it removed, only for it to come back yet again. Travis was only eighteen months old at this time. He was referred to an oncologist even though his tumors were benign. The decision was made to have Travis start chemotherapy. My one-and-a-half-year-old brother had begun a battle far greater than any I had endured.

The chemo kept the tumor at bay, but the side effects were a hefty price to pay. Travis never lost his hair, and on the whole, you wouldn't really know Travis was facing anything like that just from observing him. He was defiantly full of life and joy, and that strength even as a toddler gave us strength too. While a normal kid by most accounts, the chemo did affect him on the day he got weekly treatment. Travis would be nauseous, and all his energy would be zapped from him. An incredibly heartbreaking, confining, and sometimes even angering thing to witness as only an adolescent myself. The next day though, he would bounce back strong and be good all week until the next treatment. At three years old, Travis was taken off the chemo, believing they had eradicated the benign tumors. I'm sure you have already guessed: it came back.

Travis endured a third surgery at three years old—one surgery per year on average for his young life. The surgeon came out of the operating room with less than good news. "I couldn't get it all. The tumor is wrapping itself around Travis' facial nerve. If that nerve is severed, he would lose the ability to control half of his face." Hard news for all of us. His intravenous chemotherapy treatment continued after the surgery. Not too far along into his chemotherapy session, the oncologist had learned of new research showing that a drug developed to treat breast cancer had shown to be useful in fighting the Juvenile Fibromatosis. This form of chemo was in pill form, and the switch was made.

Upon Travis switching to the pill form chemotherapy, my mom noticed some oddities in Travis. He began having memory issues, ranging from forgetting how to get dressed to not remembering the dangers of a stove top—pretty frightening stuff. Between my mom's fastidious personality and her nurse training, she was always on top of stuff like this. She brought it to Travis' doctor's attention. Mom was met with scorn.

"None of the literature has anything about memory loss in it."

My mom is not a shy lady, and she pushed back. "As you know, this is a rare disease, and this drug is experimental in treating it. Reactions can vary, and I don't care if it's in the literature or not. This is happening to my son. We're taking him off these pills."

The doctors tried to protest, but once my mom had her

209

mind made up, it was pretty futile arguing with her. Against the recommendation of the doctors, my mom had succeeded in switching Travis back to the intravenous chemotherapy.

Travis was back on the chemo for a good while, and once again the doctors were hopeful the chemo had eradicated the tumor. After going off the chemo, a few months passed and that damn tumor came back. This time, my mom believed she was feeling a mass on the other side of his head. To this point, the tumor had only come back in that one original spot. Back on chemo Travis went. Travis then qualified for a wish from the "Make A Wish Foundation." My mom explained to him the best she could that he could make a wish. Travis wanted to meet the Power Rangers. Mom relayed the request to the foundation, and they did their best to make it happen, but ultimately fell short. They asked what else he might like. When Mom asked Travis again, all he wanted to was to meet the Power Rangers. After some coaxing, Mom got Travis' second wish—to go to Disneyworld. That wish the "Make a Wish Foundation" was able to deliver on. And, Mom being Mom—hired a Power Ranger of her own. She invited our twin cousins over around Travis' age. They had a great time—but the guy's costume wasn't quite spot on, and Travis questioned the Power Ranger over it. Mom was able to usher the faux Power Ranger out the door before the mystique was totally blown. Travis may have been acutely suspicious of that Power Ranger, but he was distracted for a moment and made some good memories with our cousins. He enjoyed his time in Disneyworld as well.

There were some scares along the way having to do with various counts of components in his blood. At one point things were looking so bad that Travis would need a blood transfusion. My mom being the hero that she was, who also happened to have the same blood type as Travis, donated her blood for the transfusions that thankfully never needed to happen. Travis went on and off chemo for the next few years—never complaining, never getting bitter, just dealing with it and moving forward. Even though he was my much younger brother, I looked up to him immensely. The one thing that had us holding on was the theory that these benign tumors grew the same way our bodies grew, so in theory, once Travis was done growing, he could potentially beat this thing.

Sixty-six

You Can Only Be So Strong for So Long

I make mention of my brother's fight because I am inspired by his strength. The last surgery Travis endured was met with the sweetest words any of us have ever heard.

"I got the whole thing," uttered Travis' surgeon.

We were all skeptical, but cautiously optimistic. Only time would tell, but that didn't keep us from hoping, praying and touching wood whenever we got the chance.

In addition to Travis' strength, I'm in complete awe of my parents' strength. I can't imagine what it must be like to care for such a sick kid afflicted with such a rare disease. It was hard enough as his brother. My mom is a strong woman and exemplifies a mama bear protecting her cubs perfectly. She was put to the test by pompous and too busy doctors, as well as fighting the schools on Travis' behalf to receive the accommodations he was entitled stemming from his fight.

Us siblings were very lucky to have the parents that we have. Kind, compassionate, smart, educated, loving, and fierce. Their medical backgrounds were more than useful, but their resolve and fighting spirit that matched Travis' were pivotal. Mom and Dad had different styles. Dad, the more stoic type, would be introspective in conceptualizing and strategizing with the specialist on this impossibly rare disease. Mom was the point person and just handled everything with a special touch that only an iron fist donning a velvet glove can achieve.

After a while, that sort of eternal high-stress environment took its toll, even for someone as strong and unwavering as my mom. Mom fell into a depression after years of valiantly battling on my sick little brother's behalf. Her youngest. Her baby. All the while my acting out took a toll on her too.

She was still fighting for Travis, as well as taking care of the rest of the family and household. With her focus so splintered, she forgot to take care of herself. It became our turn to take care of her. Dad, Cindy, and I did our best to figure out how to support her without having her feel attacked. We thought family counseling might be a good idea, and to break her the news we would all go out to dinner.

We got a babysitter for Travis and went out to dinner to broach that difficult topic with Mom. It was emotional of course, but we kept our focus on letting her know how much we loved her and how good of a job she had done taking care of all of us. It was simply our turn to take some of the weight off her shoulders and refocus the family to a more sustainable path forward. The stars aligned magically that night. It was hard for Mom to hear, but it brought us all closer together. It did feel supernatural though. After dinner and our conversation, we followed it up with a walk along the boardwalk. It just so happened that night happened to be the night we encountered the man drive into the Long Island Sound. It was as if we were meant to be there.

Sixty-seven

The Way Out

While my brother's struggle wasn't the cause of my acting out, I'm sure I hurt from his unfair circumstance—an innocent child being afflicted with such a difficult disease. I was existentially angry about it all, which only fueled my other rebellious anger. There's a saying in counseling that "the mad kid is the sad kid." Truth is, I was depressed.

One of the agreements I made with the school was to attend outside counseling, which allowed me to make up my missing work. I was resistant but saw it as a means to an end. I started those sessions much like how the protagonist Will from *Good Will Hunting* played by Matt Damon interacted with his court-mandated therapy sessions with Sean played by Robin Williams. If you haven't seen it—obstinate is the operative word. Much like Robin Williams in the movie, Arnie, my therapist, was able to eventually melt my icy demeanor. Simultaneously, my school counselor Ms. Clark was doing double duty back at high school, going to bat for me with all my teachers and administration. I can't thank Arnie or Ms. Clark enough for their help and belief in me. While both of them were the equivalent of floatation devices while I was overwhelmed and drowning—they were quite literally lifesavers.

While I saw some pinholes of light break through the dark, lonely mental space I was residing in, things were still not better with my parents. I still saw them as wholly responsible for meddling with my life, and had they just butted out, I wouldn't be in this mess. Adolescent logic and arrogance is something to marvel. My parents were beside themselves for not knowing how to help me. My dad decided to unlock his horns with mine. He tried to reason with me despite evidence pointing at the futility.

"Dave, if you had a really smart son that could do anything he put his mind to, but was throwing it all away what would *you* do?"

I wasn't ready to talk to him.

I responded with the only words I've had for him for weeks.

"Fuck you."

This time was a little different though. My dad's words sunk in. I left my room and tracked him down.

"You want to know what I would do if I had a son that could do anything he put his mind to but was squandering it?"

"Yes. Please tell me."

"I would do whatever the fuck he says, if he says he can get himself out of the hole he's in."

"What does that mean though? We're not going to do just anything you say."

"It means that when I'm making up all this work, should I need to miss a day of school to get it done that you provide me an absence note."

"OK, what else?"

"Nothing, just stay out of my way."

"That's it?"

"That's all it's ever been."

"OK then, let us know if you need anything else to help you. So long as it's reasonable."

Just then my mom, who had been listening in on the conversation, chimed in.

"Absolutely not. I'm not writing him a sick note if he's not sick."

Now my mom was the one who most of the time took care of discipline, unless we had a really serious infraction, then she'd call in the big guns of my dad. My dad was all too content with that arrangement for the most part. But, not this time.

"If our son is telling us that he can get himself out of this mess and all he needs from us is a note every now and again, you absolutely will write that note."

Being the squeaky wheel put my parents against one another, just another casualty by collateral damage. My mom protested, realizing that allowing me to win by breaking the rules was reinforcing the wrong message for me. She ultimately gave in, realizing that nothing else had worked to date. Admittedly it probably wasn't the healthiest resolution for me or any of us. But it was all we had, and it was workable. Slowly but surely, I dug my way out of that hole I had gotten myself into. If you add up all of my absences and tardy slips from my time in high school, it very nearly equals one year of missed school.

Sixty-eight

Where I Belong

Originally slated to go to an ivy league university, I blew it all in my sophomore year of high school. Truth is, if I had buckled down and redoubled my efforts I could have parlayed that into a story of triumph and it would set my application essay apart from the rest. Instead, the bar was set low, and I was content to not have to do any work to maintain a low B average. I didn't study for SATs and thought it was a badge of achievement to have still scored above average instead of what I should have felt: that I was selling myself short. I managed to get into a small but good liberal arts school, but still immature, I viewed it as beneath me. I continued my practice of doing the bare minimum. If you don't change anything, not much changes. I graduated college with a low B average as well.

I felt unfulfilled, unactualized, and embarrassed. I knew I wanted a meaningful life, and I knew I was going to have to work for it. I studied philosophy as an undergrad, and while very happy with the education, it didn't offer much in the way of direction after I was done with it. I had considered almost every career under the sun. Some of my closest friends that were living together at the time actually had a random list on the refrigerator of careers I had considered, was considering, and would likely consider. A conservative estimate of the number of careers on that list would be 30. Almost 10 more than years I had been alive. Wanting a meaningful life and to merge my intelligence with my athleticism, the best I could come up with was military officer. I was in touch with a recruiter, and I read every military memoir I could get my hands on. The one that stood out to me the most was *One Bullet Away* by Nathaniel Fick. I was so moved by it that I actually reached out to him and to his credit, he answered. He was kind to take the time to do so. Mr. Fick was more helpful than one could hope, but the decision to join the military was a weighty one. I was still lost and unsure. I was working as a personal trainer at the time, knowing the whole time it was about time I moved in the direction of what my career would be.

My smart, fun, and business savvy cousin, Eric, wasn't too keen on the idea of me joining the military. Neither were many of my friends and family members. I was on the brink of applying to officer candidates school to commission into the military when Eric made an offer I couldn't refuse. I was visiting with him for Danny's (his oldest son) Bar Mitzvah, when he floated the idea of me living with him and his family to help run and grow the nonprofit tennis camp he had started. "Look if it's not for you, you can join the military after and then we'll have the memories." It made sense to me, and I came on board.

After growing the camp 400% in one summer, we had a disagreement about compensation. I had drummed up all this business, which one might think was a good thing. Trouble was, I wasn't getting paid adequately for it, and he didn't want to do the work that all this new business created because it was just his side project. (He was able to retire at 32 after being bought out of the shares of his telemarketing company.)

Just one more side note: I worked for that telemarketing company one summer when I was still in high school. After just a couple of months, I was the number one salesman of the number one office out of 34 offices. Sorry for the bragging, but just wanted to point out that there was a history of me doing well for Eric. After realizing the tennis camp thing wasn't going to work, I began to do some serious soul-searching. Ultimately the military never felt fully right for me. I think my reasons for wanting to join were right and aligned with most young men, but at the end of the day, the jobs I was interested in (infantry officer, etc.) meant the skills I would be developing was how to get good at killing people, and that just never felt quite right.

So, if not the military then what? As mentioned before, I wanted a meaningful life. I thought back to jobs I had had before and enjoyed. Most recent at the time was helping to run the tennis camp. I had thoroughly enjoyed the travel camp counseling I had done. I came to understand I liked working with children, and that seemed pretty meaningful to me. I considered teaching, but with my degree in philosophy, that would mean I would have had to get back and earn another undergraduate degree in the subject I wanted to teach and then a graduate degree in education. That didn't feel fair or right. Upon researching further, I learned I could become a school counselor with graduate work. Counseling seemed like a better fit for me the more I thought about it.

Sixty-nine

Cockiness Slapped Out

Once I had made up my mind to pursue becoming a counselor, my focus turned to getting into graduate school. I would need to take the GRE, a test similar to the SAT to get into graduate school. Not a fun thing to prepare for or take, but a requirement nonetheless. Looking at the application schedule indicated, I would have one month to study. Before I embarked on my studying, I saw it fit to take a practice exam to see where I stood. I scored in the 40th percentile. My heart sank. That type of score on the GRE coupled with my undergraduate GPA of a 2.89. I thought to myself, *I know I'm a good student and capable, but how is anybody else going to know that?* I was quite discouraged, but I made the decision to buckle down and just do the best I could and the chips would land where they would.

I busted myself studying in that month like I had never studied before. That month passed way more quickly than my liking would have dictated. It was time to take the test. At the time, the GRE was administered on the computer with an interesting algorithm guiding the difficulty of the next question. If you got the previous question right, the next question would be harder. If you got the previous question wrong, the next question would be easier. Pretty straightforward, right? Thing is, when you're being tested like that, it means that for the entirety of your test, you are working at your capacity, right at the limit of what you know and what you don't know. This test lasted *hours.* Now, the particular test I took in the testing center just so happened to be in the suite next door to where active construction was being done. *How is this freaking possible?!* So, after hours of working at my very limit with the construction distraction next door, I finally finished the test. What was I met with at the end of the test? Only a

218

countdown timer with five minutes on it and two buttons to click: "Submit Scores" or "Cancel Scores."

If I submitted my scores, I would get to see instantly how I did, but so too would the schools that I applied to. If I canceled my scores, the schools wouldn't see the results, but neither would I.

There I was, completely spent from taking that test with construction going, facing this equally difficult decision. I began rationalizing. *That was difficult. I'm not sure I did well on that. The construction was a big distraction. Not studying for your SATs is coming back to haunt you now.* That inner voice was digging from way back and wasn't too encouraging.

I fought back though. *I studied hard. I did my best. If I didn't do well, I will be able to build on it and explain it to universities later on. I need to know how I did.* I held my breath and clicked the "Submit Scores" button. I was brought to the next screen where my score flashed immediately. I scored in the 75th percentile. I hadn't felt elation like that in a long time.

Now the 75th percentile doesn't sound quite so stellar, and a part of me was a little disappointed with the score. But, that was a huge improvement from where I was just one month earlier. Also, the program of counseling psychology I was applying to was a part of the "soft sciences." The significance of that is that the GRE is administered to students of all disciplines including the "hard sciences" like physics, etc. As it turned out a score in the 75th percentile for a "soft science" program was far above the mean. Learning this I got arrogant and only applied to the one school I wanted to go—Rutgers University. Sure, I would be accepted.

"Dear David,

While your credentials meet our requirements, we can only offer you a spot on our waitlist for the program..."

Waitlisted. I was crushed. I began hustling to get late applications into other schools, cursing my arrogance the whole time. Only after being completely humbled, and scrambling to make up for it was I accepted off the waitlist. I made a decision then and there to make the most of this opportunity. It took me longer than most to find some career direction. I saw it clearly in my head that I was on a dock of sorts and all the career ships were preparing to set sail for their various career ports of call, and I was stuck in indecision. "All aboard!" My heart rate raised. "Last call!" I still did not move. The horns blasted out, and I was still on the shore. Ships were now beginning to pull away from the docks and still I didn't move. Finally, all of the ships had set off and only then did I decide to make a break for it. Running full speed, I reached the end of the dock and leapt as far as I could. Midair time slowed, and I realized I was going to make it. I crashed into the stern of the boat as time sped back up, and I sustained a separated shoulder from the collision. Gritting my teeth, fighting through the pain, I hoisted myself up onboard. I made a point to learn the lesson. Yes, I had made it. But my hesitating had cost me. I would heal on this voyage, and I would work my way to the front of this ship and be the first off upon our landing. I would become the student I always should have been. I would treat my study with the honor and seriousness it had always deserved. School was important again.

Seventy

My Return

With all of the backstory covered, we are back to my scheduled return to my cousin's being pushed back a week. My exasperation had room to grow as I did all I could while stuck out of state. A slow week eventually passed. With my ducks in a row and my car packed, my sister volunteered to help me move back in. We traveled the one hundred miles following one another. My parents were very kind to buy me a car so that I would be able to finish my degree. It was a beautiful 21-year-old Mazda 626. Fitting name, I thought, as it was at least 626 colors of various rust. One of the rear windows needed to be tapped up—oh and you could see the road rushing by through the floorboards. Scary enough on its own, but add in the exhaust leak and the smell of gasoline, and it was a harrowing experience driving that beauty. I think pulling into handicap spots and hopping back to retrieve my walker with gawkers staring was among the most self-conscious I had felt.

My time spent ruminating over being disallowed to return brought me to a petty retribution. I decided I would in fact cash that $1,200 check with my name on it on the bulletin board. Cindy and I arrived, and she helped me unload the car. When we were done, I threw her my keys.

"Park it on the street for me please."

"Dave? Are you sure?"

"Yeah, I was told I'm not allowed to park on the driveway."

"You know that was before this, and I'm sure you're allowed to park on the driveway."

"Perhaps, but I would have thought I was welcome sooner too."

She was right I did know better. I guess I was still

making my immature point. My sister was good and did what I asked, even though she knew it was petty. Passive aggressive as I may have been, I was glad at the time to have done it—especially because that check that had been there for weeks was no longer there. Ellen was pardoning of my passive aggression and implored I park in the garage. At least until the overwhelming smell of gasoline was too much to bear. I did eventually have my spot back on the driveway though. That's something I guess.

Seventy-one

Back to School (and Work)

My classmates and professors were happy to see me in back at school. I was happy to be back too. I think I received an even warmer welcome at my internship school. My colleagues there were truly great. One fellow counselor, Rebecca, spent a little more time making sure I was comfortable. We never dated but I was keen she had a liking for me. Rebecca was the type to speak the thoughts on her mind. After she was satisfied I was on the mend, she had one more question for me.

"Dave, you know how you got that tattoo right before your accident?"

"Yep, about one month before. Pretty trippy how I was looking down at my arm and it was literally telling me to endure and persevere."

"Yeah, trippy. Just one thought: You know how our religion of Judaism disallows getting tattoos? You don't think that car accident was God's way of punishing you for that tattoo, do you?"

"No Rebecca. No God I can conceive of would put me through that because of a tattoo."

"Yeah, probably not."

"I gotta go Rebecca," I said while rolling my eyes.

But what if she was right? I don't mean it in a punitive wrathful sense, but what if he guided me to the tattoo and the accident as a way for me to help and comfort others going through difficult circumstances? An interesting thought, if nothing else.

One way I was already giving back was by volunteering with the wrestling team, and when I walker-ed into the practice room, I received a hero's welcome. I was moved—not to tears because you know, machismo. That wrestling team and its coaches were not only a welcoming crew, they were gifted and served to further humble me. When I first met the team and coaches, I was cocky thinking how excited they would be to have a mixed martial artist on the coaching staff. I thought I'd be top dog so to speak. Turns out, I was the worst wrestler on the staff. There were two all American collegiate wrestlers. The other two? One was district champ, and the other a region champion. Their wrestling prowess far outshined mine. The only thing that outshined their wrestling skill was their welcoming nature. Where I lacked their technical know-how, I was able to contribute via motivational speeches prior to meets, perhaps those speeches would have a little more behind them given what I was battling. I was happy to have that family. I was reminded how lucky I was with that welcome.

Seventy-two

A Dozen Down, A Baker's Dozen Up

Back at grad school I was pulling extra duty because of that extra class I had to take—the one all of my classmates took while I trained and fought. Extra duty, at one-quarter speed. The winter of 2011 was a particularly snowy winter in the tri-state area. In addition to having to navigate those snowy roads in my rust bucket, I had to get around once I was out of it as well. I used my walker early on. The problem with the walker was two-fold really. Firstly, I was carrying all of my weight on my hands. Actually, more than all of my weight, my fully packed backpack with books as well. I will have pain in my wrists for the rest of my life because of my extended time on that walker. The second problem was that using the walker was twice as slow than using crutches. The crutching motion allows you to swing through, covering twice the distance with each stride. Add in that you can alleviate some of the pressure from your wrists with the part of the crutch that rests under the arm—I chose to switch to less stable crutches, for better or worse.

My decision was rewarded with falling. A lot of falling. Twelve times to be exact. I counted. Each time sucked. I was falling on broken bones. One time was worse than all of the rest though. After a long day of classes and piloting my heap of junk over a windy, icy road, I made it back home to my cousin's. It was a still night. The moon was in its new phase. I stepped on black ice and went flying along with both my crutches and my regrettably not fully closed book bag. Laying on the cold ground on top of all my ringing breaks, I cried out, cursing that clear winter sky. Once I had my fill of howling at the absent moon, I collected myself, collected my scattered books, and stood up one more time.

All that struggling wasn't in vain though. I hit the ground running, or at least crutching, at a good clip. I put my pain into finishing out my degree. I received many compliments from my professors and classmates for powering through. Perhaps the best and most unexpected compliment I had ever received came by way of my former professor and co-chair of the counseling psychology department. He informed me that he had nominated me to deliver the commencement speech. Blown away, and completely humbled, I thanked him profusely. There were seven others nominated, and a committee would make their selection based on the speeches themselves. We would have to write our speech and then perform it for the committee via video recording. Just another thing added to my already overflowing plate. Overwhelmed by the nomination and the added work, I got to grinding.

Seventy-three

Learning to Trust Again

It was a few months of getting around on walker and crutches before Dr. Popowitz gave the all clear to start putting weight on my leg again. As excited by the news that my healing was on track and even ahead of schedule, it wasn't as exciting as the prospect of beginning physical therapy. Physical therapy meant that I would be able to have a direct role in my recovery. You know, apart from drinking gallons of milk.

First thing was first though. That first step months after my leg being shattered was the single scariest thing I would have to voluntarily face. While I got the news in Dr. Popowitz's office that I could begin to weight-bear, I waited until I got back to my home at my cousin's before attempting. Furthermore, the familiar and comfortable surroundings weren't enough. I didn't tell my cousin or his family about my clearance. In fact, I waited until I was home alone to take that scary first step. Using one crutch and the island in the kitchen for support, I first rested my broken leg on the ground. No pain yet. I began to slowly distribute the weight from my good leg over to the injured one. Once about 20% of the weight had been transferred over, my leg made clear I was still injured. I clenched my teeth and pushed for more. Slowly and incrementally I added more and more weight to that hurt leg with pain increasing at an exponential rate. I could feel the beads of sweat forming around my temples. I pushed through the pain further, more confident in Dr. Popowitz's promise my leg was ready for it than from the feedback I was getting from my own limb. I put in 45%, 46%, 47%, 48%. Those beads of sweat graduated to streams pouring off my face. I kept going—49% then finally 50%! I did it. I was standing on both legs each carrying half of my weight. I threw down the crutch and let go of the island. I was standing on my own two feet for the first time since this whole ordeal had begun. I wasn't satisfied though. To walk would mean that the leg would need to be able to carry all 100% of my weight as my other leg swung forward for the next step. After standing there for a minute or so, my sweat turned cold as I prepared to take my first true step. After some self-rallying, I swung my bad leg forward and just went for it. With the different densities of my femur and the titanium rod running through it, it felt like sparks shooting off from the friction. I shorted it a bit, rushing my good leg forward to retake the responsibilities of carrying my weight. It wasn't pretty, but I had done it. I took my first step in relearning how to walk again. Figuring I had done enough for my first attempt, I collected my crutches and went on about my day. It would be sometime before I would make any such attempts in front of anyone.

Seventy-four

Unbridled Excitement

One of the main office secretaries at the high school I was completing my internship at made a strong recommendation for a physical therapist that had helped her son-in-law recover from a car accident, albeit leaving him with less serious injuries than mine. Her raving over the months my bone was healing was enough for me. I scheduled my first appointment.

I was met by a physical therapist, Michael, a friendly and boisterous man who spoke with an Eastern European accent. After filling out all of the paperwork, I crutched over to hand it in.

"Very good David. I will be right over so we can fill out the intake survey together. This is to establish a baseline starting point for the work we will embark on together."

Michael sat down across for me. He distributed the survey to me with a copy in front him as well. Before going through the survey, my own excitement got the better of me.

"Michael, it's so great to meet you. You come highly recommended by one of my colleagues. I am so excited to start this process. It's been months with only a passive engagement in my own healing. This marks the beginning journey back to fighting mixed martial arts again," I rattled off at a million miles per hour.

Michael's retort in his thick accent was an effort to calm me down. "David, relax. We are only doing the intake interview and survey today."

"I understand. While this may only be a survey and interview to you, this is a very important milestone to me. I will stop at nothing to come back to a hundred percent."

"OK David I get it. Let's start the survey."

I don't think he did get it, but I was happy to start the process. That survey revealed my leg was at 30% capacity. My heart sank a little. Michael could tell.

"Relax David. We have to start somewhere."

Seventy-five

Disappointment

After suffering through lugging my broken body to and fro through the snow, uphill both ways (ha ha), to finish out my master's degree, I made it. You might be wondering, *Whatever happened to that commencement speech nomination?* After pouring my heart and soul into it, I was confronted with bitter rejection. My speech was not selected. Instead, I would come to learn that the Provost in charge of the speech selection chose her own student out of the seven nominees. Doing my best to remain open and trying not be consumed by sourness, I gave the commencement speaker the benefit of the doubt. *Surely it will be a good speech, and her being the Provost's student will be merely coincidental,* I thought to myself. Nope. It was more or a less a Woo College! type speech. That was incredibly hard to sit through, knowing what I had a written. Perhaps I was biased though. Either way, I spent all that time writing it, and my family who graciously attended my commencement were further charitable to listen to me speak my speech after the ceremony back at my cousin's. I guess I'm still a little salty about it even to this day, but truth is, had I been selected that may have satisfied me on some level, potentially keeping me from writing this book. I guess that's one example of how not getting what we want might actually be better so long as we fail forward, both learning from and using our failures to fuel our next greatest success. Anyway, you be the judge if I was being petty. Woo College! or this:

I owe a huge thank-you to my adviser, my professors, and the Rutgers Graduate School of Education as a whole for all of the lessons taught, all of the support given, and this opportunity to address the Graduate School of Education's 2011 graduates and their families. Congratulations fellow graduates on the culmination of all your hard work and dedication. And congratulations to our parents, for I know if your parents are like mine, they've earned this day just as much as we have, and in the case of my parents, maybe even a little more. I am truly grateful to walk at this commencement ceremony with all of you. Heck, I'm really happy just to be able to walk.

Four short months ago I was quite literally blindsided. A truck slammed through my tiny two-seat sports car, fracturing my pelvis in five places and cracking my femur (the big bone in my leg) right in half. I am truly happy to be alive, and in some strange way I am even happy for that accident. For you see, along with the challenges it has dealt, the accident also bared a few gifts. Coming that close to death has opened my eyes to life like never before. Priorities fall fast in order and one's perspective on what is truly important comes clearly into focus.

Love before anything else is what's truly important. Allow me to assure you that everything else falls dim when love shines bright. I sincerely wish for the infinite warmth of love to bathe every one of you throughout the entirety of your lives. I now know that I was taking my time here for granted. Please let my close call free you to love more freely. Now with my priorities set straight after love, comes work, but not just any work. Work in the way of service to others. While I was lying in my hospital bed after surviving that horrible crash and awaiting surgery with all of its inherent risks, I found myself praying, yet not merely for my life or my limb. I was praying to be looked over and protected in order for the chance to do what I now clearly see as my life's work: helping others. One of the reasons that my experience here at the Rutgers Graduate School of Education has been so great is because I am surrounded by intelligent, inspiring, and selfless people that share the value of helping others. From the students to the faculty and staff, there is a passionate idealistic energy infused with our learnings and our fieldwork. Some say it is naïve to be idealistic, but I respectfully disagree and hope that we hold on to our idealism.

Lastly, my crash experience reminded me how important it is to go for your passions. As we embark on the beginning of our careers, a large part of our jobs in education is providing the tools for our students to reach their dreams. On this day when we are recognizing you and your achievement, I encourage you to keep dreaming and going after your own goals. For, by dreaming and working for those dreams, you serve as inspiration for students going after theirs. There is also a certain authenticity gained when students see you fully engaged in life. Here may be the best news of all: love, service, and the pursuit of our dreams are not mutually exclusive. Rather, there is synergy when we weave all of them together in our lives. The clarity my crash brought me has been my greatest blessing in disguise. I hope sharing my experience was meaningful and gives you inspiration to live well and help others do the same. I must thank all my friends and family for your love and support in helping me live my dreams. Graduates, congratulations again; it has been a true honor to learn by your side. I wish everyone here love, fulfillment in your work, and the realization of your dreams. Thank you.

Seventy-six

Faith

I was extremely grateful to have my family support me by coming to my graduation. There was a hard truth I learned from their presence. My joyful Uncle Jerry and warm Aunt Hilary, were able to spot me in the crowd. It's not that they spotted me that was upsetting of course, rather it was the means in which they did so—my pronounced limp.

Physical therapy was certainly working. Considering my starting point, one might be satisfied with the progress that was made in a relatively short time. Not I. Don't get me wrong, I was thankful that I was making progress, but the end goal of fighting again was still far off. I treated physical therapy like a religion. I went three times per week without fail. I did everything they told me to do both in and out of session. We were progressing. Albeit slowly. While my bones continued to heal, the associated pain was also beginning to subside. However, there was a new pain that was starting to emerge. The outer part of my hip would get sore after each physical therapy session. Being an athlete my whole life, I had become acutely aware of my body and could easily tell the difference from a soreness derived from working out vs. a soreness that was injurious in nature. This pain was the latter.

A few more months had elapsed, and I had earned not my first, but second long-term leave replacement school counseling job in the high school I had done my internship. I also began fighting a lawsuit against New York State for that recently demoted park ranger's improper action. All the while physical therapy continued. I worked my leg back to almost 100% competency. I was surprising the physical therapy staff by throwing spinning kicks and flying knee strikes. The staff saw my range of motion and athletic prowess and placed me above the general (uninjured) population. There were two things that kept up my own determination of reaching that 100% mark. The first being that I could tell through a pain in my leg that it was going to rain before anyone else. I think it had to do with the differing densities between my leg and the titanium rod and the changing barometric pressure undergoing different rates of change on bone and titanium. Not the end of the world, and something I was willing to live with. The other more distressing remnant from the accident was that if I were to go for a short run, one mile at the most, my upper leg would be so irritated that I was relegated back to limping for three days after such a short run. The physical therapists believed that rod was protruding beyond the end of the bone, rubbing against the soft tissue in my upper leg. I went back to Dr.

Popowitz, and the x-rays were inconclusive. I was faced with a difficult choice: live life mostly as if it never happened, really only limited by the inability to run—or go back under the knife to remove the rod down the center of the femur, which the bone had been growing around, where it was intended to stay. I was informed that while unlikely, I was risking the bone being broken all over again and having to start the process of healing from scratch. The odds were a 70% chance of no issue and a 30% chance of complications. A difficult decision, no doubt. But, I couldn't fight the way I was, nor would I ever be able to. With that, I elected for the second surgery in the hopes of attaining that 100% recuperation.

Almost exactly a year after the car accident, I went in for my second operation. All I can say is, "Damn all that milk." What I once credited for my unnatural healing and bone growth was now working against me. Once in surgery, Dr. Popowitz quickly observed how my bone had grown and latched onto the titanium rod. I was in surgery hours longer than scheduled. Dr. Popowitz wrestled with taking that rod out of my leg for all of those hours. Have I mentioned how much of a godsend Dr. Popowitz was? I was rewarded for all of his toiling with an unbroken, rod-free femur again. I was back to 100% just me. Turns out, my Wolverine-esque body rejected the adamantium. I would be on crutches for a few more weeks, and I would need more physical therapy, but I could finally see the light at the end of the tunnel.

Seventy-seven

Summoning Strength

As if recovering from a second surgery wasn't difficult enough, I was also at the tail end of my second school counseling leave replacement position and already hired for my full-time position. One of the responsibilities of a school counselor was helping seniors submit their college applications. Part of that meant I had to write recommendation letters for those students to submit with the rest of their applications.

Our school had a policy that we needed 10 business days to process the college applications. Leading up to that second surgery, I was working on a stack of those applications. While working on the submitted applications, I would inevitably receive more from stragglers that were past due. The first students to submit their applications for me to process were the high-achieving type who got their work in well before the college's deadline. Being green in the field, I was trying to do it all. When the stragglers came to me after our deadline and last minute for the college deadlines, I took it upon myself to work on the more pressing applications, pushing back the early submissions. I was susceptible to having my heartstrings tugged on, and over-confident I could get it all done. I didn't miss a single college deadline, but some of the early submitters' applications got pushed to the back of the line because their college application deadlines were later. Thing is, high-achieving students often have helicopter parents, and when they found out their student's application weren't submitted yet, despite there being plenty of time left for the college's deadline—they brought it to my boss' attention.

Of course, the shit hit the fan at the worst possible time—as usually it does. My boss called me right after I was out of surgery to chew me out. Instead of fighting back, I let him know how I got myself in the predicament (after all it was with the best of intentions to help the stragglers out), and busted myself to get everything done from my hospital bed.

What started out as a mistake of mine could have been made worse if I had gotten defensive, or if I made an excuse because I was laid up. Instead, I committed to putting my head down to do the best I could from that point forward. What would come of it was out of my control—I just did the best I could after making a series of mistakes. And, it paid off—whereas my boss' high opinion of me had fallen given my naïve mistake, it was not only restored by meeting the challenge and facing my mistake, but my boss eventually came to boast about how I did all that work from my hospital bed. I turned a mistake into an asset by admitting it first and doing all I could to correct it at an inopportune time of my healing, with no guarantee I would be able to get all the work in on time or save my reputation. I just did the best I could, and as it's been my experience, good things tend to follow, albeit sometimes taking longer than I'd like.

Seventy-eight

Afghan Hound in the Rocky Mountains

I recommitted my efforts into physical therapy after that second surgery. After just a couple of months, I had achieved the first part of my goal. I was good as new. It was as if that the car accident never happened. It was bittersweet to leave physical therapy. Sweet because after working as hard as I did for as long as I did, while maintaining my focus and faith, it all worked out. Bitter because I became friends with all of the physical therapy staff, and they were integral to putting me back together. At the very end, Michael approached me to say goodbye and wish me well. Before he could say anything, I began to thank him sincerely for all the help and support he had provided. He gave a curt nod of acknowledgment and then in that thick accent of his, he confessed something to me.

"David, when you first crutched through these doors, and you were overly excited wanting to get the physical therapy underway, you told me that you wanted to fight again. I've been doing this for a long time and given the nature of your injuries and the shape you were in at the first meeting, I thought there was no way you would ever walk without a limp again, much less fight. I saw my job as to minimize the impact of the car crash had on you. But, then I got to know you. The spirit you brought to your healing, even in the face of setbacks rejuvenated my own jaded perspective. I speak for all of the staff here; your energy has uplifted us all. It is me who should be thanking you. Thank you. Make sure you to let me know when you fight again; we will all be there."

We've all heard before how a positive attitude can help us heal. I believed it, and not only did it help me, it helped those around me who were there to help me. I was quite literally revitalized, and I poured that back into training again.

"If it ain't broke, don't fix it." Once back training, instead of going through the proper channels (Brian) to book my next fight, I simply just got back in touch with Scott, the boisterous promoter.

"Hey Scott."

"Hello, who is this?"

"It's Meanberg."

"Holy Shit! Meanberg! How the hell are you?"

"Good man, I've been through the wringer; came back from a serious car accident, but what's important is that I'm back."

"Glad to hear your all good. What can I do you for?"

"Well, to mark that I'm fully back and that I haven't lost a step. I want to fight and win again."

"I hear you. I guess you don't know: I folded up the promotion. Too many shady characters in this business."

"Oh, sorry to hear, Scott. Would you be able to point me in the right direction for a different promotion then?"

"They're all shady, kid. Tell you what: I'll put some thought into it and get back to you." I thanked Scott, but I didn't think he would really go through any trouble as there was nothing in it for him. I kept my focus on my training.

I had been moved out of my cousin Eric's house for some time. He had always been a force of generosity in my life, and he continued the trend. He offered to take me skiing in Vail, Colorado to celebrate my full recovery. Having procured my new full-time position in the new high school meant our schedules were slightly disentangled, meaning I had to meet him out there. This was a guys' trip of sorts—my two cousins about 15 years older than me (Eric and Ira), and each brought a son about 15 years younger than me (Ethan and Ian). By the time my flight landed in Denver, they had already been out there for a couple of days. I rented a car and headed off for Vail, two hours away through some gorgeous mountain passes. On my way to meet up with my cousins, my phone rang displaying an unfamiliar number.

"Hello?"

"Yo! Meanberg! How are you doing?!"

"Hey Scott, doing well! What's up? Do you have a fight promoter you can recommend me to?"

"Better. You've inspired me. I started up my promotion again, and we're going to Philadelphia, and you're going to headline! Well, if you want to, that is."

"Are you serious?! Of course, I want in! Thank you, thank you, thank you!"

"Don't thank me kid. You're the reason for all of this. I have some connections out that way, and the plan is to get you and your comeback story all over the media to blow this thing up!"

"That's awesome Scott. Thank you, man. I don't know if you remember that I had about a hundred supporters show up last time."

"Oh, I remember kid, counting on you to deliver that again."

"Scott, no exaggeration—for this comeback fight it'll be double that."

"OK kid, I'm going to hold you to that."

"Deal."

"OK kid, I gotta go. Tons of work to do now. You'll hear from me soon."

"OK Scott. Thanks again."

Perhaps inspired by my picturesque surroundings, I took a deep breath and thought to myself, *Wow, there really is something to this positive thinking when met with hard work. Those forces together can move mountains.*

Seventy-nine

~~Twelve~~ Thirteen Down

The timeline of my fight training overlapped with my best buddy's wedding. John and Melissa would be getting married soon, and John cordially asked me to be his best man. With it came a few duties. A speech (perhaps a shot at redemption, at least I didn't have to audition for this one), and a bachelor party. I took both responsibilities very seriously. First up the bachelor party.

It would be in Montreal. I planned dinners, nightlife, and activities. The dinners were swanky and tasty. The nightlife was tame; we were still nerds after all. The activities were fun and memorable. We went go-karting, paintballing, and skydiving. One was more memorable than the rest, at least for me. And perhaps not the one you might guess.

In the middle of one of the games of paintball, I found myself up on top of a turret shooting down on my friends. As the battle intensified and I was taking fire, or paint more accurately, I began to run on top of the turret, evading those raining paintballs. Now I'm not a complete idiot and was using the railing in my peripheral vision to guide my action. When the railing stopped, I would stop running. A sound plan I thought. Trouble was, my plan didn't account for the cutout in the floor. Honestly, who puts a cutout in the floor of a paintball turret? One instant I was running, and the next I was in freefall. My martial arts practice of learning how to fall came in handy as the spill I took was 10 feet. I absorbed some of the fall with one hand. Unfortunately, it happened to be the hand that was wielding the paintball gun. My index finger caught the trigger guard. The rest of the fall was concentrated on my lower back. I got to my feet and heard my friend rounding the corner. He took a few shots at me. I evaded and returned fire, then took him out. Right afterward, I decided it was silly for me to keep playing—I had a fight I was training for. I had to fight so hard just to get back the ability to fight. I sat the next couple of rounds out and iced my finger. I was reasonably sure it wasn't broken, but there would be no way I would let it stop me even if it was broken anyway.

We all made it back to the hotel to shower off the paint before going out that night. My back started to feel tight after my shower, but I put it out of my mind. We made it to our dinner reservation. Over the course of dinner, my back started getting tighter and tighter. Then that tightness turned to pain. The pain turned tortuous. One of the French-speaking waiters saw the discomfort I was in and brought some loose pills over for me. After some pantomiming, it was understood and he brought pills over for my back. Shrugging my shoulders, I slung them back, calculating the unmarked pills were worth the risk given the pain I was in. I was glad I took those pills because even with them, when I stood for the first time, I was in the most pain I had been since that car accident. Worse than any of those dozen falls on my broken bones even. I went back to the hotel with our one friend who was finishing up medical school, while the rest of the crew took John out.

The next day was our last day. Of course, I tried to schedule the best for last. We were to go skydiving that last day and then would drive back to NYC from Montreal. I could no longer stand up straight. I had never been skydiving and wanted to go really badly. Furthermore, my $300 deposit was nonrefundable, even though I was the one who had booked them for our entire party. Still, I made the responsible decision to not join the rest of my friends and was relegated to watching them for my $300. Hard as it was to be sidelined, what was to come next was far worse.

Halfway back on the drive home, I lost motion in my

left foot. When I got to my parents' house, I demonstrated my paralysis for them. With the concerned looks on their faces, I knew that I had indeed lost my comeback fight. My dad made some phone calls to his friends and colleagues to get me seen that next day. Here I was again undergoing more MRIs and the like. That 10-foot spill directly on my spine herniated four discs in my spinal column. I was told surgery wasn't necessary at this point and that over time, the peripheral nerves in the area would take over control of the blocked nerves being pinched by my injury. In short, I would need to have more faith that my body would heal from another devastating injury.

I called Scott to break him the news.

"Meanberg! How the hell are you? How is training going for the fight?"

"I've got bad news, Scott."

I didn't want to tell him how it happened. I felt like it would come off as irresponsible that I was playing paintball while in training for a fight. I told him I fell from a height and shared that I had four herniated discs in my spine and that my foot was paralyzed. What was to come next, I could have never guessed or been prepared for.

"Are you fucking kidding me?! You have to be kidding!"

"I'm not kidding Scott. I'm really sorry."

"You can't do this to me. I put my entire life savings into restarting this promotion. I was counting on you and your supporters to make this work! You can't do this!"

"I'm really sorry Scott, but I obviously can't fight with these injuries and being partially paralyzed."

"You've ruined me. You've absolutely ruined me! Do me a favor kid, if you heal from this one don't call me again. Goodbye!"

"I'm sorry Scott. Good—" *Click.*

He hung up before I could finish. *Great.* Just what I needed. The guilt of ruining a man's livelihood on top of my new injury. I know now, as I knew then, that his over-commitment wasn't my fault, but it still didn't feel good. It still doesn't.

Eighty

Fourteen Up

The body is an amazing thing. No surgery was needed after all. It took about one year to regain full use of my foot. It was a slow process where I got incrementally more and more control over my foot over that year. My body was one thing, but what was unforeseen for me was the depression I fell into after not being able to answer the bell of my comeback fight.

My friends and family, as supportive as they've been through all of my challenges, struggled to understand why this got me so down. I had come back from so much. This latest injury was nowhere near as bad as the car accident. What they were missing was that my aim to get back into the cage is what got me through the injuries from the car accident. Some friends and family even employed tough love on me to try and nudge me out of the depression. It didn't work.

John, who had been a bedrock of support since we had been 10 years old, was particularly hard on me. I tried to let him in on what it was that I was going through. I had read the New York Times article, "Athletes' Injuries Go Beyond the Physical." It really resonated with me. Some of the salient points:

"A month after badly breaking her left leg and blowing out her right knee in a skiing crash in Switzerland, Picabo Street, the fearless, spunky media darling of the 1998 Nagano Olympics, shut herself in the bedroom of her parents' house and closed the blinds. She would not let family or friends in, she took no phone calls, did not watch television, did nothing for weeks but lie there in the darkened

241

room thinking miserable thoughts. 'I went through a huge depression,' Ms. Street said. 'I went all the way to rock bottom. I never thought that I ever would experience anything like that in my life.'..."

"...Dr. Deborah Saint-Phard, who treats patients at the Women's Sports Medicine Center of the Hospital for Special Surgery in Manhattan said, 'There's a pervasive sense that athletes are superhuman, not only in their abilities to perform athletically, but also in their morals, their ability to handle pain, disappointment and injury.'..."

"...Picabo Street came out of her depression and her bedroom on Mother's Day, and has now resumed training for competition. 'I had gone over the pessimism so many times that it got old and boring and I needed something else to go over,' she said. 'So I started thinking about what I had to be thankful for. What I came to was how much my family loves and supports me. After four hours of hashing it out, I got up and opened the door.' That was the first step toward becoming her old, cheerful self. 'I just had to force myself every day to focus on the things that were good, even though it was so easy to think of all the things that were bad,' she said."

I sent John the article and his well-meaning response back to me was, "I got up and opened the door." He missed the point (along with the rest of the people in my life). Like Picabo, I needed to do it on my time, when I was ready—no one could rush that. Eventually I did get up and open my own door, on my terms.

While I did find my way forward out of that darkness, I never did get that comeback fight. Instead, I transitioned my focus to harnessing all of the challenges I have faced to write this very book, in the hope it should help others surmount their own. Admittedly there is part of me that feels there is some unfinished business in need of tending. Perhaps another fight is still in order, followed by another motivational tale.

The End (of Act I)

Epilogue

I think few would argue that I've faced my fair share of obstacles. This book is among them. One challenge related to this book was actually to select which challenges to include. I have written more than double than what actually made it into this book. I had to learn how to write a book as I was writing it. Strictly workwise, this has been the most difficult endeavor I have ever undertaken. It took tremendous discipline to keep plugging away—which required a constant internal battle with myself. I have struggled with procrastination my whole life, and a project such as this did not align well with that flaw. There were many times while writing this that I thought I had bitten off more than I could chew. That I was not good enough. That I would not be good enough. I battled [myself] on.

"But all things excellent are as difficult as they are rare," said Spinoza. As difficult as this project has been for me, that difficulty itself was my north star telling me I was doing something worthwhile and hopefully at least in the direction of something excellent.

As if this most difficult work wasn't enough, it was all within the context of the rest of my life. And, life doesn't stop. Just a small sampling of what has happened while writing this book:

1. My brother's illness threatened its reemergence—thank God it was a false alarm
2. Fought a lawsuit against New York State and won a settlement

3. My grandmother broke her femur and told me one of the things that helped get her through, was the example I set through recovering from my own broken femur
4. Became trapped on a glacier alone and suffered minor injuries including frostbite
5. Was told by a police officer in the West of the USA that he almost shot me. Why? I was driving 10 mph over the speed limit
6. Had my laptop stolen
7. Won a poker tournament in Las Vegas—the first one I had ever played in
8. Contracted poison oak from head to toe, so bad that it made me wish for the frostbite back
9. My best friends John and Melissa underwent a divorce
10. Worst of all, I suffered a betrayal by someone I trusted among the most in this world

That betrayal was the most painful thing I have ever been through. And as you now know, I've been through a painful thing or two. Like in combat, it's the blows that you don't see that hurt you the worst. When I was dropped by those thugs defending my friend Adam, the shot that dropped me in the cage, heck, even when I got hit in the car accident, I had to endure some of the worst damages I have sustained. What they all have in common is that I didn't see them coming. The reason why betrayal hit me so hard was because it was a blow that I not only didn't see coming, but it came from a direction that I was sure a blow wouldn't come from. This person had led me to believe they had my back no matter what.

When a blow comes from the very person you trusted to protect you, it sends you into an existential crisis. You question everything: who you can trust, what you can trust, even if you can trust yourself. How can anyone be expected to trust anyone or anything after that happens? I don't know. But, what I do know is that we must learn to, or we'll perish. Worse, we'll have to learn to do it with the knowledge that that pain exists and can come out of nowhere. Simply not trusting is no way though.

Perhaps the worst part of the betrayal was that it threw me down a hole I had never been in. It was only through returning to my study of psychology with a concentration on betrayal did I come to learn that betrayal was a different sort of a hole to be trapped in. In all of my other challenges, I hit rock bottom and built up and out. Betrayal is a bottomless hole, and worse I didn't know it—so I kept falling. Learning that it was bottomless shook me to my core. It scared me to death.

Once over my fear, I realized it was on me to slow and stop my descent by any means necessary. I clawed at the walls of the hole I had been knocked down to stop my descent. After expending a tremendous amount of energy to merely stop falling, I then looked up and saw how far I had to climb. Further than I ever had to get out of any other hole. I was already exhausted, but I took a deep breath and started to make my way towards the light. There were many slips as I worked my way up and out. That's ok though, slips are inevitable—it's how we react to the slips. If we throw our hands up and give in to the slip saying, "What's the point?" we give up all that hard-fought progress.

The betrayal hit me particularly hard for a couple of reasons: 1) I attributed the source of so many of my achievements to having been blessed with a great support network, and now I couldn't trust it like I had. And 2) While writing this book to hopefully help inspire people out of their holes, I felt like a phony because I was trapped in a hole that I couldn't get out of myself. Who was I to help anyone out of a hole when I was stuck in one? I was pushed forward by the goal of helping people. That goal is bigger than me. I had to find a way to heal so I could help others. After having experienced among the most physical pain a human can feel, I can unequivocally state that emotional pain is far worse than the worst physical pain. I also think it's more common.

On some level, I am happy for all of the "bad" things that have happened to me. I have been given opportunities to see what I'm made of, to show there is no quit in me in fighting for what's right, even if I need to take a break from time to time. Those challenges have steeled me for each subsequent challenge. On some level, I'm happy to have gone through the betrayal as it has steeled me even further. Odd as it is to say that I'm thankful for the car accident and everything else too. I *never* want to have to go through any of it again, but of all the things I have faced, it was the betrayal that brought me to my knees. Maybe that's why it had to happen: for me to learn no matter how willing and able I am to face some of the most difficult challenges, there are still some things that I have no control over.

This portion was the hardest to write by far. I was knocked down a deep and lonely well by someone who had my full trust. It was a challenge to relay all of the good deeds and qualities of that person in this book. Betrayal not only steals your trust from the present moment, but it also has you questioning the authenticity of past events. I am back from that horrid hole, and I can tell you there is a way out. The way out is not to betray your own morals no matter how deserving someone is of your wrath. The difficult thing is often the right thing. If it were fated for me to be knocked down into the underworld, you'd best believe I was going to retrieve this book from its depths to help prevent others from having to take this same trip. Much like saving that guy in his car, I was not coming up without this book.

Like my trainer's wise words after that first round of my life where I never took a beating so bad "Sit down! Shut up! You're gonna win this thing!" even when I had no reason to believe it. I have done my best to apply that to these other challenges I have faced, but that is not why I selected it for the title. It's for you, the reader. You might be going through something tough with no apparent reason to believe you will come through it, but Sit down, shut up, **YOU**'re gonna win this thing.

One more thing: I am still discovering my own spirituality, and in no way do I want to push my limited understanding and belief on others. I believe there is something bigger than all of us. Whether you call that God or the universe or the laws of nature is personal and your own business. To take a step back from that and use a child's understanding of what God might be like—a white-bearded, all-knowing and all-good figure in the clouds might help me to get my last point across. If that simplified version of God had come to me and said, "David, I need you to save a man by pulling him out of a submerged vehicle, rise from being shattered, rise again from being paralyzed, save your friend from five beasts, struggle in your vocation, suffer at the hands of someone you love and trust with your whole heart, etc. etc.…" I think I would have responded, "God I will do my best, but I think you have the wrong man. I cannot do *all* of that."

And what is crazy about that, is I would have been wrong. We are all far more capable than we give ourselves credit for.

Acknowledgments

This book would not have been possible without the love, support, and patience of a great many of people. I am eternally grateful to those who supported me at the time of my accidents and throughout my corresponding recoveries. I am equally appreciative to all those that offered their hand up to help me through my down times. I have much love for you all. The obstacles I have overcome with your support has directly enabled the writing of this book.

To Mom and Dad: I couldn't have asked for a better set of parents. You are both loving, wise, and encouraging. You instilled in me the values of doing the right thing and doing my best. You taught me I could achieve anything I put my mind to, and I just happened to be crazy enough to believe you.

To my siblings: Travis, even though you are my baby brother I catch myself looking up to you, as you bravely battle the challenges laid at your feet. You never complain, you just take it all in stride. You would make the Stoics proud. Cindy, we've been through so much together. May you live honorably and prosper from it.

To Grandma: You inspire me more than words can convey. Thank you for your patience through our many talks where you have imparted much wisdom, spirituality, and joy. I will treasure all of it, along with our many laughs forever.

To John: My brother from another mother. We have both been through the wringer countless times. I couldn't imagine making through any of it without your friendship and support. "…sometimes you're ahead, sometimes you're behind. The race is long, and in the end, it's only with yourself."

To Uncle Pete: You have the patience of a saint to charitably tutor me through this writing discipline. I hope I have not embarrassed you too terribly with my amateurish prose. It would seem I am much more predisposed to bashing things out than tarting them up. Pax vobiscuits.

To Ira and Eric: Better mentors there are not. I look up to the both of you in awe. I am grateful and a lucky man to glean a mere fraction of your collective sagacity. Well, that and there is no one else I would laugh harder with during a nut shot battle.

To my large and zany extended family: I wouldn't trade any of our crazy and loving times for the world. Though I make many mistakes and have fallen many times, you have always been there to catch me in your loving arms. Thank you a ton.

To all of my dear friends that have become family: your love and support has truly helped to carry me through tragedies. Especially when I was faltering in my own belief I would make it through. All the while doing your best to quell my inflated ego in the in between. I am so fortunate to have each one of you in my life.

To my loved ones that have passed on: I carry your love and spirit within me. You help guide me when I am lost, give me strength when I am weak, and protect me from malevolence (and from myself).

To the first responders and healthcare professionals: thank you to the ones who took such great care of me, put me back together, and rehabbed me back to full health. You are all angels on Earth. Special thanks to Dr. Popowitz.

To Ms. Clark: Superhero is the only thing that comes to

mind as you helped me through many concurrent difficult situations. Ill-equipped to handle them on my own, I am not sure where I would be today if it were not for you.

To all of my coaches, trainers, and training partners: Thank you for making me a better version of myself. You helped steel me, to endure and prevail over the many challenges that would come.

To the haters and betrayers: Read it and weep.

Made in the USA
Columbia, SC
18 September 2018